Hospital Supporting Services & Systems

Brig. (Dr.) M.A. George

2010

DAYA PUBLISHING HOUSE

Delhi - 110 035

ISBN 81-7035-653-9
ISBN 978-81-7035-653-0

Published by : **Daya Publishing House**
1123/74, Deva Ram Park
Tri Nagar, Delhi - 110 035
Phone: 27383999
Fax: (011) 23260116
e-mail : dayabooks@vsnl.com
website : www.dayabooks.com

Showroom : 4760-61/23, Ansari Road, Darya Ganj,
New Delhi - 110 002
Phone: 23245578, 23244987

Laser Typesetting : **Classic Computer Services**
Delhi - 110 035

Printed at : **Chawla Offset Printers**
Delhi - 110 052

PRINTED IN INDIA

Preface

There have been many books written about the clinical aspect and medical and professional systems of a hospital, which is as it should be, because this deals directly with the main functional aspect of the hospital. But what is not so well described is the supporting systems of the hospital, that contributes to a large extent to the success of the hospital. The CEO who mostly leads the hospital, being a physician, gives undue importance to the clinical professional function of the hospital, putting the supporting systems on the back burner. As a Medical Director in a number of large super specialty hospitals, for considerable time, I have to plead guilty to this omission with serious consequences to the functioning of my hospitals. It is this realization that has prompted me, to write this book.

In this book Hospital Supporting Systems like Pharmacy, Lab, Imaging services including X-ray, Blood

Bank, Hospital Dietary Services, Mortuary, Hospital Fire fighting services, Hospital Laundry, Bio Medical waste disposal etc has been dealt with in detail. Space requirement, construction imperatives, lighting, staffing and so on has been dealt with from a functional and practical angle. This book will be vital for Hospital Governing Bodies, Hospital CEOs, Medical Directors, Hospital Administrators, and students of Hospital Administration.

Brig. (Dr.) M.A. George

Contents

Introduction

The sick and injured go to a hospital, to get cured, and if this is not possible, to at least get their ailment alleviated and their pain reduced. The unit that carries out this function is the medical team, headed by a medical professional who has a recognized qualification in medicine. This team works in the ambience and environment of a hospital, this ambience and environment helping them to achieve a favorable clinical outcome, in the optimum time. The successful hospital, success being estimated by the quality of medical care it provides to its patients, has a well built scientifically designed structure, in which integrated clinical departments function, with the support of other non-clinical systems. The clinical aspect of medical care, and the medical and professional systems of the hospital, has been dealt with, in detail, in many books written on the subject, quite correctly too, because these deal directly with the main functional aspect of the hospital. But what is not so well documented or described, or rather neglected, are the Supporting Systems of the hospital, which contributes to a large extent, to the success of the hospital. It is the physician who heads a hospital as The Chief Executive, and naturally he gives undue importance to the clinical professional aspect of the hospital functioning, putting the Supporting Systems on the back burner. As a Medical Director of many large super specialty hospitals, I am guilty of this mistake, and this had serious adverse consequences, in the functioning of my hospitals. It is this guilt and realization that has compelled me to write this book.

The ground realty in an Indian hospital is, that the "Doctor", is first among the hospital hierarchy, and so other professionals, equally qualified and skilled in their subjects like Management, Human Resources and Finance, have to take a secondary position to that of the Doctor. This prevents the good among the non medical professionals, from making the hospitals their career, at great loss to the hospitals. This in turn prevents the hospitals from achieving their full potential. There has been considerable improvement in this regard in the last decade in India but this anomaly sadly continues to exist.

This book is to bring to the notice of the top hierarchy of hospitals, and hospital administrators the needs, functions and the specifications of the Hospital Supporting Services. Such awareness will bring more attention to these services, and consequent increased resource allocation to this area, which in turn will enable the hospitals to achieve their full potential. This may be the right place to pause and define the specific departments which fall within the term Hospital Supporting Services. As the designation suggests, these departments and services provide support to the medical team, to bring about an optimal clinical out come. Broadly these can be divide into Supporting Services, and Supporting Systems. The usual departments designated as supporting services are, Pharmacy, Laboratory, Radiological and Imaging Services, Central Sterile Supply Department (CSSD), Physiotherapy, Blood Bank, Medical Records Department (MRD), Hospital Dietary Service, Hospital Laundry, Hospital Mortuary, and Transport Section including Ambulances. The supporting systems include Fire Prevention, Hospital Engineering Services, Hospital Security Section, Hospital Public Relations, Hospital Marketing, Hospital Waste Disposal, Hospital Infection Control, Medical Ethics, Hospital Material Management, Laws Applicable to Hospitals, and Quality Assurance System. These departments, systems and sections are interrelated, and fully integrated with the hospital clinical systems and departments. But for convenience of description, they are being dealt with separately.

Brig. (Dr.) M.A. George

Chapter 1
Pharmacy

The premier supporting service of the hospital is the Pharmacy. The purpose of the Pharmacy is to provide the correct medicine, in the correct dosage, to the correct patient, at the correct time. In order to do this, the pharmacy has to procure, stock, and dispense (distribute), the required drugs to the Outpatient and Inpatient attending the hospital. The importance of the Pharmacy can be gauged by the fact that, 25 per cent of the cost of running a hospital is incurred by this department. The amount spent by the pharmacy, is second only, to that of the expenditure spent towards salary and wages. Moreover Pharmacy accounts for more than half of the total hospital material costs.

Location and Space

The ground floor is the preferred location of the Pharmacy, with easy access to the Outpatient department, the Casualty, and the Inpatient area. Its location should provide that the patients after collecting their medicines exit the hospital, without coming back into the hospital reducing patient cross traffic. When it comes to the space required for the Pharmacy, though the rational space requirements have been worked out, it is a pity that in most Indian Hospitals, it is based mostly on the area existing in other hospitals, and is ad-hoc in nature. The result is that the pharmacy is too small or too large. The rational method, agreed upon by consensus is, to first calculate the OPD attendance for each session of OPD, assuming that there is a morning and evening OP. In India, we have to add one or two bystanders per patient to cater to the prevailing social practice, the number of bystanders being more in rural areas. In this calculation, the space required is 0.8 sq m per attendance. For those who want ready reckoners and rule of the thumb the following rule can be used-

- Minimum-23 sq m
- For hospitals of 100 to 200 beds–0.93 sq m per hospital bed.
- For hospitals above 200 beds–0.50 sq m per hospital bed.

The preferred layout of the main pharmacy is in the form of a rectangular hall with various counters located there. The waiting area is in front of these counters. In addition, you must have arrangements for cool storage in the form of dark rooms, arrangements for cold storage, area to receive bulk stores and break it down, as well as an administrative office for the in charge of the pharmacy, with arrangements for storing documents.

Objectives of the Pharmacy

The objectives of the pharmacy can be summarized as under-

1. Make available drugs for OP and IP patients, which are done by purchasing, storing and dispensing.
2. Ensure storage under optimum conditions, so that the quality does not deteriorate during storage.
3. Follow and adhere to the rules and regulations of the Drugs Control Act, as applicable.
4. Ensure high professional standards of the pharmacists employed.
5. Exercise financial control in the management of drugs and dressings.
6. Promote rational drug therapy.
7. Act as a profit center of the Hospital.

Drugs and Therapeutic Committee

The effective function of a hospital pharmacy will depend to a large extent on good communication between it and the clinical services. The above committee is meant to meet this requirement. This committee must be compact, with the Medical Director heading it, or if there is no medical director, a designated senior clinician heading it. The chief pharmacist is its secretary, and the Heads of the Clinical Departments are to be invited to attend its meetings, on an as required basis. The functions of the committee are-

1. Prepare the Hospital Formulary.
2. Select a panel of suppliers

3. Lay down a pharmacy policy and make the users aware and conversant with this policy.
4. Developing a Drug Information Center.
5. Monitoring adverse drug reactions.

Hospital Formulary

With hundreds of formulations, and thousands of manufacturers, identifying quality drugs is no easy task. To assist the physician in ensuring rational prescribing of drugs, the hospital formulary plays a significant role. Some important points to be borne in mind are:

- ☆ It must be acceptable to the medical staff, specially the clinicians. To ensure this the clinicians must be involved in preparation of the formulary.
- ☆ Generic as well as brand names must be indicated.
- ☆ It must be reviewed at least once a month, for additions and deletions.
- ☆ Must be based on WHO list of drugs
- ☆ Once the formulary is accepted, only those drugs contained in it must be prescribed and stocked.

Drug Information Center

It is the job of the Medical Representatives to increase the sales of their companies by highlighting the superiority of the drugs of their company. So collection of the correct data and passing it to the users becomes imperative. The best way to do it is to earmark a space, where scientific literature can be displayed, with easy access to the doctors. Responsibility to organize and keep it updated is to be given to the chief pharmacist, supervised by the Therapeutic Committee.

Inventory Management

Unless there is proper inventory management, the hospital will end up holding medicines which are not required, and not stocking medicines which are required. The ingredients of inventory management are:

Purchases

All purchases must be centralized, and from a list of selected suppliers, the list being updated periodically. All purchases must be in writing, and as per a laid down Purchase Performa. If a telephone order is given in an emergency, it must be followed up by a written order. While ABC analyses is good, the appropriate analyses for a pharmacy is VED analyses, that is Vital, Essential and Desirable drugs, and holding reserves accordingly. All supplies must be accompanied by a bill, it must be matched with the purchase orders, and if there is a shortage, a shortage note must be initiated. If a drug which has not been ordered is supplied, it must be rejected and a rejection note initiated. After the supply is tallied, it must be entered into a stock book and the entries verified again. If stock is computerized, a print out must be verified with the bills.

Inventory

There is always a problem to determine the quantity of stock to be held. There are seasonal variations in demand, and so you may have to workout the requirements season wise. The best method is to study the pattern for the last three years. But if this is difficult, you can work on the average expenditure for the last year and add 10 per cent to it. But it is imperative that a scientific system be used in determining the requirement. Unless you have a proper system to work out the requirement, the system will fail.

Re-ordering

Before you determine the re-order level, you must decide on a policy on how much reserve you must hold. The reserves will depend upon whether the item is vital, essential or desirable as determined by the VED analysis. This also will depend on the lead time that is the time taken on ordering, to the time of actual delivery. It will be shorter in urban areas compared to the rural areas and will differ from state to state. Then you work out the average monthly expenditure for the various seasons. The monthly re-order level will be this average plus the reserve. Once this is entered into your computer system, it will indicate the items and quantity you have to order, for the ensuing period. If it is not computerized, the rule is that, once you touch the reserve, which is kept separately on the shelf, you re-order.

Storage

Most of the drugs can be stored under atmospheric conditions. But some have to be stored in a cool room, rooms where the sun rays do not enter fully, meaning dark rooms. Some of the drugs have to be kept in cold storage, in Frigidaire, which must have alternate generator back up. The important point to note is that nursing stations must be given a list of items which are to be kept in cold storage so that they don't leave these drugs in the open. This is specially in regard to sera and vaccines.

Turnover

Even with the utmost diligence, some drugs remain on the shelf without being used, these being termed as "slow moving" drugs. Once in three months, it must be identified, and the doctors must be requested to prescribe them, in preference to similar drugs. If this does not work, the stock has to be returned to the supplier, and a credit note obtained.

Stock Display

After considerable experimentation, the consensus is to group the drugs into tablets, injections, syrups, dressings etc and then display it on the shelves in the alphabetic order of the group. Different hospitals can adopt different methods. On the rack, the reserve is to be kept at the back with a divider, and the drugs in use are displayed by keeping the drugs with the shortest life in front, so that they are used first. When fresh stocks are received, the reserve must be turned over, so that it has drugs with the longest life.

Time Expired Drugs

The computer program must have a provision to indicate the drugs which has only six months life left. Then it is evaluated, whether it can be used within its life period by a reference to the average expenditure. Those that cannot be used within the life period, is to be returned to the supplier, and a credit note is to be obtained.

Pilferage

This is one of the most annoying problems in a pharmacy and must be dealt with harshly. There should be no access to the pharmacy by unauthorized persons, the pharmacists must leave their handbags outside while entering the pharmacy, and no item must be taken out including departmental issues, without a cash bill or a credit bill. Loss of attractive items must be dealt as one of pilferage, and dealt with accordingly.

Dispensing or Issue

The whole purpose of the pharmacy as stated earlier, is to ensure that the correct drug reach the correct patient, in the correct time, at the correct dosage. Hospitals may devise different methods of dispensing, but certain cardinal principles must be adhered to.

OP Patients

It is preferable that the dispensing is done directly from the doctor's prescription, rather than it being copied into another slip. The usual two methods are that the case chart is passed to the pharmacy, or as the doctor writes the prescription, a carbon copy is made and one copy is passed to the pharmacy. The latter is preferred.

The method used for routine dispensing is that the items are taken out from the shelf, placed on the counter, the bill is made, and cash received. Then the chart or prescription is passed to the dispensing counter. Here the drugs are checked with the bill and prescription, put in paper envelops, and dosage written on them. Before handing over, the name and address of the patient is again checked, to ensure that there is no mistake, because the names are the same.

IP Patients

The ideal method is to take the drugs to the nursing station and dispense from there, but it involves meticulous planning and the staff sticking to the plan. The more usual method is for the bystander to bring the prescription to the pharmacy. The method of issue is same as that of OP Patients.

Staffing Pattern

The number of pharmacists would depend upon the workload and size of the hospital. The consensus is that a hospital must have a minimum of one pharmacist for a 10 bedded hospital, the number increasing by one for each 100 beds. In addition, these pharmacists can be supported by pharmacy assistants at the scale of one assistant per pharmacist. Duties of cashier and store keeper must be performed by non technical persons. Of course, the number of counters will play an important role, in this context.

Equipment

The type of equipment for storing and display of drugs in a pharmacy has undergone many changes. But the best system of storing drugs, especially in India still remain the open ended steel shelves. In addition tables, chairs, stools, filing cabinets, and steel cupboards with locking devices, will be required. Narcotic drugs will have to be kept under lock and key, by the doctor who holds the license for narcotic drugs.

Pricing of Drugs

The principle is that rates charged, should at least ensure that the costs and overheads are covered. The simplest method is to stick to the maximum retail price (MRP), given on the packing of the drug, which now includes taxes and amount payable under VAT. It must be remembered that even charging one paisa above MRP is a criminal offence, and will attract harsh penalties.

Legal Implications

The legal requirements is covered by the various regulations and orders issued on the subject. In India Health is a State subject and so there may be differences between states to states. However in most states, the large hospitals now obtain a license from the State Drug Controller or an equivalent authority, for their pharmacy. But, some hold that hospital pharmacies do not require a license, if run under the direct supervision of a Doctor. Their rationale is that hospital pharmacies, do not sell drugs, but only dispense them as part of the treatment.

In most states, orders exist that stocking of narcotic drugs require a special license, such licenses being issues in the personal name of a qualified doctor. The hospital must keep a close liaison with the office of the State Controller and its branches in the various states, so that they are familiar with the current orders.

Chapter 2

Laboratory Services (LAB)

Present day medical practice is to a large extent dependent on investigation results provided by the Lab. At present there is an overdependence on the Lab, it being used for diagnosis, rather than for confirming the diagnosis made by clinical evaluation. The Lab is also one of the important profit centers, generating more income for investment as compared to other departments. The Lab investigations are ordered to confirm diagnosis, monitor progress, and facilitate follow up. It is invaluable for managing emergency cases, and so its services must be available round the clock, especially in clinical pathology, biochemistry, and microbiology. The technical progress in the area of Lab is dramatic, but the Lab administration has not kept pace, and so, it is an area for hospital administration to focus on.

Workload

In the 20th century, a medical case underwent 20 lab investigations for a hospital stay of 10 days, averaging 2 tests per day, per case. Today the tests done for the same period is almost 60, averaging 6 tests per day, a three fold increase. In addition to the increase in the number of tests done, there is a doubling in the kind of tests done, indicating a phenomenal increase in the workload of the Hospital Labs. But a surprising fact is, that a small variety of tests form, almost 70 per cent of the total tests done. A study by an Indian Army Pathologist has identified these tests as hemoglobin, total and differential leukocyte count (TLC and DLC), erythrocyte sedimentation rate (ESR), blood sugar, blood urea, blood cholesterol and urine cum stool analyses. This has to be born in mind while planning the LAB.

Functional Structure

The Lab is functionally divided into Clinical Pathology (Laboratory Medicine), Microbiology, Hematology, Histopathology, Biochemistry, and Urine cum Stool analyses. The usual problem when setting up a new Lab, or modifying an existing one is, that the Pathologist or Lab technician who is entrusted with the job, tries to duplicate one in which he has worked, or copy one which exists in another "modern" hospital. This must be discouraged as the old mistakes are copied, and the correct method is for the hospital administrator, the architect, the pathologist and the Lab technician to sit together and work out a detailed plan, including the internal arrangements.

Location

The earlier concept of having the lab in the ground floor is not valid anymore, as the collection of samples is done at a separate collecting point in the OP, or collected from wards and taken to the Lab. However the practice of the ward nursing staff collecting the blood samples has now been replaced with the Lab staff collecting the same from the wards. The exception is that daily urine samples of diabetic patients are collected and tested in a suitable place in the ward, by the ward nursing staff. There has been a recent dispute in Kerala among house surgeons and nurses as to who will collect the blood samples. The correct person is neither, but the lab staff.

Centralization versus De-centralization

There has been continuous debate whether the Lab resources should be centralized or decentralized, especially in large hospitals, both having its supporters. Centralization has the advantage of optimum utilization of resources, routine tests being done more economically by "batching", and lending itself to automation. The disadvantage is that samples have to be meticulously tagged and transported, and large volumes may jeopardize quality. On the other hand decentralization has the advantage of quick availability of results, less inconvenience to patients, and better service to the critically ill patients. Its disadvantages are that, it is uneconomical, difficult to automate, and difficult to control and supervise.

Space Requirement

The Lab space is calculated in terms of Laboratory Space Unit (LSU). The LSU does not mean separate rooms but only area measuring 20x10 ft, giving 200 sq ft (about 18.6 sq m). The rectangular pattern has been chosen, as it will have more bays and so is compact. The space requirement can broadly be divided into:

1. Primary Space for technical work.
2. Secondary space for administrative work.
3. Circulation space for uncluttered movement of personnel and equipment.

At a rough estimation, the space for a hospital of 200 to 300 beds would be primary space of 20 LSUs, that is about 372 sq m, and the secondary space being a little more. Approximately, the circulation space is 10 per cent of the total of primary and secondary spaces.

The layout is becoming less rigid, due to increasing automation. The administrative area is separated from the technical area, so that access to technical area is only for the technical staff. The administrative area contains office, the sample collecting area, the bill and cash counters, and the waiting areas for the patients. Adjacent to the waiting area is a vene-puncture cubicle, where blood is collected, and the waiting area is provided with a toilet or toilets for collecting samples of urine.

Systems for gas, water and compressed air should be so located, so that they are easily accessible from the outside. One way of doing this is to arrange the Lab benches, at right angles to the walls, and to provide removable panels. Waste water pipes must be of non corrosive material.

Staffing

A large Lab is headed by a Pathologist who must be an employee of the hospital. But smaller Laboratories can be headed by a senior Medical Lab Technician (MLT). If controlled by a MLT, the work of the Lab must be supervised by the Medical Director or Medical Superintend.

The MLT works under the technical supervision of the senior MLT. Moreover Lab assistants are also used to assist MLT for the sake of economy. The amount of tests an MLT can do in a day would also depend upon the kind of tests he does. So the total tests that a MLT can do, calculated by work studies and by actual performance, differ, but the consensus is that a MLT can do 35 to 40 routine tests per day, while the lab assistant can do 30 routine tests per day. To ensure optimum use of technical man power, non-technical persons must be used for administrative work, documentation and for transporting specimens from the collecting point to the main Lab. Under utilization as well as over utilization of the technical staff of the hospital, is uneconomical and affects the quality of the work of the lab.

Equipment

More and more automation is the rule of the day. This high technology equipment is costly and involves high maintenance costs. However a wise investment on Lab equipment gives more return, than in other departments. But the choice must be on rational considerations and not for prestige. For example a semi-automatic analyzer for a small Lab makes more sense than a fully automated one.

Working Surface

The working surface must be stain proof and resistant to chemicals. This can be by granite, stainless steel or high density vinyl. The flooring must be acid resistant, and can be of granite or vinyl.

Internal Arrangements

Work Benches

Traditionally Lab work is done on work benches, by technicians sitting on stools with or without back rests, and is still the best option. The optimum height for the benches is 75 cm and width is 60 cm. Continuing benches allowing 2 meters per technician, is advocated. For hematology and bacteriology, staining sinks are built into the work benches. A service spine runs behind the work bench but not attached to it, containing plumbing, electrical lines and gas pipes. The work bench must be so located to enable access to the spine from out side.

Lighting

Natural light obtained by arranging the work benches parallel to the windows, is the best. But this is to be backed by fluorescent lights suitably placed. Each work bench should also be provided with a electric and power socket.

Storage Space

Considerable amount of reagents, chemicals and glassware has to be stored. Over bench shelving, under bench drawers and shelves, cupboards and movable trolleys are the usual methods adopted.

Air Conditioning

The idea is to provide a dust free environment and so central air conditioning of at least the technical area, is recommended. Exhaust fans with fixed windows, with rubber lining around the window panes, is an inferior alternative.

Procedures

Lab Sample Collection

Most hospitals adopt the method of the wards collecting samples for IP patients and sending it to the main Lab. While this is adequate for urine and stool samples, blood collection from the wards must be by the Lab staff. For OP patients, samples are collected at the OP collecting point by the Lab. Instructions for preparing patients for specimen collection, should be displayed in easily understandable language. Collection of cash for lab tests must be streamlined, so that patients or their bystanders do not have to run around.

Records

A daily register containing the tests done and the results must be maintained by the Lab, preferably on computer. Lab tests are done based on requisitions, and the results are made in duplicate, one being sent to the ward for inpatients, and to the MRD for OP patients, to be attached to the records. The duplicate copy is retained by the Lab. The time is not far, when written Lab Requisitions and reports will not be seen, the staff doing the requisitioning on line, and the reports also given on line.

A time limit must be laid down for giving the reports, and this must be strictly adhered to. Emergency reports must be given promptly, in one hour without waiting for "batching". Interpretation of results must be by senior residents.

Safety Precautions

When samples, especially blood samples are taken, it must be assumed that the patient is HIV positive and strict universal protection procedures must be adopted. Mouth pippeting is totally banned.

Some of the important precautions while collecting blood are given below:

- ✰ Only disposable syringes must be used for blood collection. Use thick dressing pads or absorbable cotton, below the forearm when drawing blood from the elbow veins.
- ✰ Do not remove needle from the syringe.
- ✰ Tourniquet must be removed before the needle is withdrawn, and used needles should never be capped.
- ✰ Used syringes and needles must be placed in puncture resistant container having disinfectants.
- ✰ Wash hands with soap and water before and after each blood collection.
- ✰ All staff of Lab must be immunized against Hepatitis-B.
- ✰ All potentially contaminated materials as a result of blood collection must be autoclaved before disposal.
- ✰ Use, disposable screw capped vials, for blood collection.
- ✰ In the event of a needle prick, immediately wash with soap and running water. Use tincture of iodine dressing. Collect blood from patient after getting consent for testing of HIV and Hepatitis-B, and give it for testing.

Waste Disposal

Lab waste especially from histopathology and microbiology sections must be treated as hazardous, and dealt with as per rules pertaining to bio medical waste.

Interrelationship with Other Departments

The Lab must establish good relations with the user departments and clinicians. The usual problem is the demand for Lab investigation of emergency cases. Even if the demand for urgency is misplaced, the Lab must understand the stress of the treating doctor, who is dealing with life and death situations, and co-operate, and later sort things out. The lab must accept that it exists for the patient and not vice versa.

Chapter 3
Imaging Services

The old X-ray department tucked away in a corner of the hospital has been replaced by the Department of Imaging Services. In addition to Radiology we have now Ultrasonography (USG), CT scan, MRI, and Nuclear scanning. Radiology itself now consists of Radio Diagnosis, Radio Therapy, and Interventional Radiology. The other noticeable change is the importance that the Imaging Services have gained in the area of investigations. Radiology is not only equal now to Lab tests, but surpasses it. In Cardiology Cardiac Doppler and Angioplasty is now competing with non interventional methods. The services of the Imaging Services should be around the clock and the rates should be displayed at the entry. Arrangements to receive cash at the X-ray department will avoid considerable inconvenience to the patients. One point to be given particular attention is, that when procedures are done female attendant must be present. It se from the electricity department as ment for prevention of Radiation

...ology

Many of the radiology departments, even in new built hospitals suffer from lack of space. It must cater for X-ray, Intravenous pyelogram (IVP), Ultrasound, and C-Arm. However almost 80 per cent of the work load is, routine X-rays.

Location

It should be located, so as to be easily accessible to OP, Casualty, and Wards. The preferred location is on the ground floor either as a separate wing or as a limb to the ground floor structure. The lay out should avoid cross traffic and bottlenecks.

Space

The WHO stipulation for X-ray department is a minimum of 20 to 30 sq m. Our studies have arrived at the following area for the X-ray department:

1. Upto100 beds: 70 sq m
2. 100 to 199 beds: 175 sq m.
3. 200 to 299 beds: 375 sq m.
4. 300 to 399 beds: 500 sq m.
5. 400 to 499 beds: 650 sq m.

Distribution of the total space, is as under:

1. X-ray rooms: 25 per cent
2. Film processing: 10 per cent

3. Administration: 30 per cent
4. Waiting area: 5 per cent
5. Circulation: 30 per cent

X-ray Rooms

These rooms form the vital part of the Radiology department. Their number will depend on the work load, and the number of special investigation undertaken. Individual rooms should be rectangular in size and about 20 sq m. The floor must be able to take heavy loads, up to 200 kg per meter. Now the developing of X-rays is not done in the old dark rooms but by automatic developing and drying machines. Each X-ray room must have changing cubicle within the room itself, with the control panel, as far away from the X-ray tube as possible, and screened by a lead impregnated screen. Doors and windows would require to be lead lined. The walls also must be extra thick to avoid costly lead lining.

Administration

The administrative areas include patient waiting room, the radiologist's office, and X-ray record room where X-rays are stored. Filing of X-rays must be done in a methodical manner, so that accessing and retrieval is easy. The radiologist room must have a number of viewing boxes. Cases must normally be by appointment. In large hospitals, X-rays may have to be stored on magnetic discs. Measures to deal with any reactions to the use of radiological contrast media should be available.

Types of X-ray Machines

They are described in term of mA, like 100 mA, 200 mA and so on. The higher the mA the lesser the exposure time and better the image, but the cost goes up steeply. The hospital will also require portable X-ray machines of 30 mA.

Staff

There are so many variables in the requirement of X-ray technicians, and so only an approximation is possible. The yard stick available is that an X-ray technician can take about 30 routine X-rays per day, special procedures resulting in less number per day. We have worked out a process of calculation which has been found effective and is as under:

- ☆ The average total daily OP load of the specialties is worked out, separately for new admissions and old cases (repeat visits).
- ☆ 15 per cent of the new and 10 per cent of the old cases will require X-rays.
- ☆ Work out the total X-ray load and add 30 per cent of this figure for I P patients. Divide this by the average routine X-ray work which an X-ray technician can do, which is 30.
- ☆ The resultant figure gives the X-ray technicians required for the day. Add 30 per cent of this figure for the night shift, the total giving the hospital requirement.

Protective measures include lead impregnated aprons and gloves, and they have to be provided on a generous scale. The staff must also wear the radiation dosimeters provided by the Atomic Research Center designated by the government. These dosimeters must be sent to the evaluation authority every month, with the control provided. If the meter indicates that the individual has been exposed to a dose more than what is stipulated, the technician has to be taken off duty for the laid down period.

Ultrasonography (USG)

This has come into more frequent use and its use is increasing. The Color Doppler has become routine investigation in cardiology cases. The clarity of the picture will depend upon the machine and so there can be no compromise on this. The standard size of the USG room should not be less than 16 sq m. and must be air conditioned, with a dressing cubicle and an attached toilet. The procedure is done by the sonographist himself with the help of an attendant. The administrative back up is provided by the radiology department.

CT Scan

It is now becoming almost as frequent as X-rays. It requires the technical expertise of a qualified CT Technician.

Magnetic Image Resonance (MRI)

The patient is placed in a high magnetic field, and the radio frequency signals are fed into a computer, which converts the signals into three dimensional images on a TV screen.

Special Points

Because of the hazardous nature of radiation and its importance in dealing with critically patients, following points to be borne in mind:

- ✩ The radiology department including special services like CT scan has to function round the

- ☆ There must be facility for doctors to view wet films.
- ☆ The dosimeter must be worn while on duty, and sent each month for evaluation. Any increase in laid down exposure dose, must be acted upon promptly.
- ☆ Arrangement to recover silver from the used developer solution must be made, as it is an added income to the department.

Chapter 4
Central Sterile Supply Department (CSSD)

CSSD are the services in the hospital, which receives, stores, processes, sterilizes, distributes and control sterile supplies, to all departments of the hospital, for the care and safety of the patients. The concept of CSSD, and central sterlization rose from the experience of World War II. Centrilization increases efficiency, results in economy in use of equipment, and ensures supervision and control. CSSD is an absolute must in hospitals conducting surgery. The major responsibility of CSSD includes processing and sterilization of needles, syringes, rubber goods (gloves, catheter and tubing), surgical instruments, treatment trays and sets, dressings and so on. This involves calculation of the total requirement of these items, and is about four or five times of the average daily use. The main function of CSSD is to supply of sterile instruments and dressings to wards and department, sterilization of instruments and linen for OT and to impart training in sterilization techniques to the hospital staff. The categories of articles dealt by CSSD can be broadly divided into contaminated, clean and sterile. Contaminated items are reusable instruments and items, which have been used. Clean articles are those which have been cleaned or reusable items which have been exposed, but not actually used. Sterilized items are those which have been sterilized, and are within the stipulated life. The point is that these categories should not be mixed, and should not be carried in the same trolley.

Work Flow

The structural internal arrangements in the CSSD, should confirm to the work flow, for the sake of economy. The work flow is receiving, washing, drying, accounting, sorting, packing, sterilization, sterile storage, and issue of sterilized articles. The articles must move in one direction from receipt to issue. The space required is 5 to 6 sq ft (1.62 sq m), per bed.

It must be easily accessible to OT, and be in close proximity to it, so that the OT matron can exercise supervision.

Facilities and Equipment

The basic working spaces is workbenches, about 89 cm high, about 60 cm wide, with waterproof and stain proof surface, as well as foot rails and stools with back rest for sitting. Thin poly foam material to deaden sound and minimize breakages, is preferable. It must have glove processing area with pile up and packaging area. The sterilization is done by autoclaves, which use saturated steam under pressure. The minimum time required for autoclaving is 15 minutes, at 121 degrees centigrade, and under 15 pounds pressure. Quicker sterilization can be achieved by raising the temperature. A needle flushing device must be used before needles are sterilized. Ethylene oxide is being increasingly used for sterilization of moisture sensitivity items like rubber and plastic. The latest is ultrasound cleaners which bombard items with sound waves.

The usual items dealt with in CSSD are, instruments, appliances, dressings, sponges, OT linen, packs, gauze and cotton, gloves, bowls, as well as trays. Kraft paper is preferred for packing than linen. Auto clave tapes are used to monitor effectiveness of autoclaving.

A minimum of four persons will be required in the CSSD. The most economical method is to give in-house training to nursing assistants or nursing aids. Strict supervision at every stage of work is absolutely necessary.

Standardization

As the process and supply is centralized, standardization is inevitable. The most economical method for OT is to have packs for general instruments and dressings, and have separate packs for specialized surgery, which can be merged at the time of surgery. But packs for commonly used sets like suturing set, vein cut down set, catheter set, incision and drainage set etc must be standardized. Standard packs for these are now available in the market.

Once sterilized, the packs are only sterile for a particular length of time. This is called the "shelf life" of the pack, and must be standardized in consultation with a bacteriologist. If the pack is not used within the scheduled period, it should again be autoclaved without opening it. But in the absence of the bacteriologist, the rule is that unused packs should be again autoclaved after two weeks.

Distribution System

There are three methods of distribution as under:

1. *Clean Exchange*: Sterilized packs are issued in lieu of used ones and are simplest.
2. *Basket System*: The user's requirement for a particular period is laid down. At a stipulated period, the basket with the items is given to the user, and the basket with the unused items with the user, is taken back.
3. *Topping-up System*: Pre-determined levels are laid down. At particular intervals the CSSD supplies the deficient items.

Whatever the system, it must be laid down in writing, and all users must be made aware of the exchange system, especially whether the user will come to the CSSD or vice versa. It is more economical for the CSSD to work only one shift, but this involves that additional packs will have to be kept in casualty for emergency use.

Chapter 5
Physiotherapy

The four pillars of Medical care are curative care, preventive care, rehabilitation and medical education. Rehabilitation is equally important as curative care, as a working man has to go back to his job, after being cured. Rehabilitation is making a clinically cured patient, functionally viable, so that he can do his work. It is evident that it is important from the economic point of view. The department of physiotherapy, which is under the control of a qualified therapist, carries out this component, as well as playing a part in the curative and treatment process. Physiotherapy is of the utmost importance in Orthopedics, Neurology, Cardio pulmonary cases, Geriatrics and Pediatric specialties and so it is located near these departments.

Physiotherapy existed even in ancient times. Physicians like Hippocrates and Hector are supposed to be the first practitioners of Physiotherapy. They used massage and hydrotherapy in treatment. The present day physiotherapy is concerned with identifying and maximizing quality of life and movement potential, within the sphere of promotion, prevention, treatment, habilitation and re-habilitation. Physiotherapy is a health profession, which provides services to maintain and restore maximum movement, and functional ability. This includes intervention when movement and functional ability is threatened by aging, injury, disease or environmental factors.

Sections

It consists of different sections, which are mentioned below:

- ☆ Reception-cum-office
- ☆ Administration area including office of the physiotherapist.
- ☆ Physical and suspension therapy.
- ☆ Diathermy.
- ☆ Ultra violet.
- ☆ Infra red.
- ☆ Gymnasium.
- ☆ Waiting room.
- ☆ Changing rooms separately for men and women.
- ☆ Toilets separately for men and women.

Space Requirement

The space requirement is given below:

- ☆ Physical therapy – 7.45 sq m
- ☆ Suspension therapy – 8.35 sq ft
- ☆ Diathermy – 7.45 sq m
- ☆ Ultraviolet–7.45 sq m
- ☆ For combined use – 7.45 sq m
- ☆ Infra Red – 7.45 sq m
- ☆ Radiant Heat–7.45 sq m
- ☆ Gymnasium – 8.35 sq m
- ☆ Waiting room – 37 sq m

Administration area including:

- ☆ Physiotherapist – 14 sq m
- ☆ Toilet – two – 3.35 sq m each
- ☆ Office cum reception – 9.3 sq m

Occupational Therapy

This is strictly not a part of physiotherapy but is closely associated with it. It is concerned with promoting health and well being. Its primary goal is to enable people to participate in the activities of everyday life. The health profession of Occupational therapy as we know it, was started in 1910 for the care of the "invalids". It works through a process, or sequence of actions called Occupational therapy process. It is based on the concept of giving people the "skill for the job of living", necessary for "living life to its fullest extent".

It is concerned with areas of School children (autism, and emotional and behavioral disturbances), post trauma injuries like brain and spinal cord injuries, home health (Alzheimer's disease), and in hospital OP (hand therapy).

Chapter 6
Blood Bank

The blood bank is the unit that carries out the operations for collection, storage, processing and distribution of blood, and its components, safely and adequately. The bank does this by collecting blood from eligible blood donors. These banks have to obtain a license from the designated authority, usually the Drug Controller, under the Drug and Cosmetic Act. This license has to be renewed periodically. Separate license is required for providing blood components.

Blood Bank Medical Officer

The blood bank is under the control of a medical officer who has undergone a recognized training in blood banking. The In Charge is responsible for the daily activities of the bank, and supervision of the other staff of the blood bank. He is also responsible for laying down policies, standing procedures, quality control and administration. It is also his responsibility to ensure that whole blood collected, processed and supplied conforms to the standards laid down. Currently blood has to be tested after collection, for HIV I, HIVII, Hepatitis B, VDRL and Malaria Parasite. The results have to be recorded on the label of the container.

Location

Should be located as a separate wing or annex. Space requirement is about 100 sq m, with an additional 50 sq m if components are prepared. It should have provision for air conditioned space for blood collection, for blood component separation, testing lab, and for refreshment cum resting room for donors. It also requires rooms for reception, sterilization cum washing, and store cum record room.

Staff

The requirement is for a trained medical officer, blood bank technician, registered nurse with training in blood banking, technical supervisor if blood components are prepared, and a lab technician.

Equipment

The essential requirements are temperature recorder, refrigerated centrifuge, heamatocritic centrifuge, general laboratory centrifuge, automated blood typing machine, haemo-globinometer, refractometer, weighing machine, water bath, autoclave, serological rotators, lab thermometers, electronic thermometer, blood agitators etc. These equipments should be kept in running condition, standardized frequently and calibrated periodically. The refrigeration must have a generator back up.

Consumable supplies like testing reagents/kits should be kept in a clean environment, and at the appropriate temperature. The principle of FIFO (First In First Out) should be adopted, so that expiry of life of these drugs is avoided.

Functioning

The blood bank functions under the rules made under the Drugs and Cosmetic Act as amended from time to time. Standard Operating Procedures (SOP) should be developed and revised periodically. These standard operating procedures must include blood collection, processing, testing, compatibility, storage, transportation of blood for distribution, autologus transfusions, donor suitability, and donor qualifying tests, donor referral, adverse reaction management, record keeping and quality control. The staff must be trained and given refresher training in these SOPs.

Records

These records are laid down by the licensing authority. The mandatory records are Blood Donor record, Master Register for blood, issue register, register for components supplied, record of ACD/CPD bags, cross match register, adverse reaction record, and stock book. The label of the blood bags are also prescribed, with color coding for different groups.

Procedures

The technical procedure details are given in the drugs and cosmetic act as amended from time to time.

Biosafety

Immunization against hepatitis must be up-to-date for all staff of the blood bank. The universal protection measures against HIV should be fully complied with. The disposal of blood bank waste must be as per Bio Medical Waste Rules. All HIV, Hepatitis, VDRL and Malaria positive blood, and hemolysed blood should be disposed off under strict supervision as per laid down rules together with their blood bags. It must be remembered that blood is tested after collection. Time barred blood bags should be incinerated.

Ensuring bio safety of blood supplied by Blood Banks, is the legal responsibility of such Banks, and any deficiency will attract punishment.

Blood Donation Camps

Such camps should preferably be within the hospital. Such camps outside the institution can usually only be held by a licensed government blood bank or the Red Cross Society. This is being revised and the provisions are being made more liberal. However the rules may vary from state to state. Hospitals must be careful not to associate themselves with blood donation camps held by private agencies especially in the less medically aware states. However there is no objection, to these parties holding blood group detection camps to draw up a blood donor panel.

Chapter 7
Medical Records Department (MRD)

This department has become an essential Hospital Supporting Service, and a vital part of all modern hospitals. The dictum is "People forget, but Records remember". Medical Records has become a specialty in its own right, and the Medical Record Officers and Medical Record Technicians have earned the right to be considered as specialist in their own field. This is so because patient care requires a chronological record of patient care and treatment, and this enables the clinical team, as well as the hospital administrator, to evaluate the quality of medical care, and the effectiveness of the hospital services. In the present day environment of considerable litigation in hospital practice, its importance cannot be exaggerated.

The medical record is defined as a clinical, administrative and legal document, relating to patients care, in which, sufficient data is written in sequence of events, to justify the diagnosis, warrant the treatment provided, and the results achieved. It can be summarized that the medical record gives the who, why and when, of the patient care.

Objectives

Its objectives are three fold namely to protect the patient, help and protect the health professional, and to safeguard the interests of the hospital. They are:

- To help in patient care management, by providing the treating doctor the personal and medical details of the patient.
- To help the patient in claiming insurance benefits, workman's compensation, re-imbursement of medical bills etc.
- To help in quality evaluation of hospital services.
- To form the basis of medical audit.
- Provide effective communication within the medical team.
- To provide a basis for medico-legal cases.
- To help in medical education and research.
- To provide data for public health.
- To generate hospital statistical data.
- To compile and intimate legally mandatory reports like birth and death reports, notification of communicable diseases etc.

Classification

Medical records are broadly divided into two, Personal records and Impersonal records. Personal records are those records which contain personal data of the patient, and which can identify him. Impersonal records do not contain the personal data and so the patient cannot be identified by a reference to it. The importance of this classification is that, the personal record cannot be made available to others, without the permission of the patient, or the authorized next of kin, if the patient is dead. But the impersonal record, without details of personal identification, can be made available, without such consent, for research, medical education or for collating statistical data.

The permission to release the information in the personal records must be obtained in writing, and if it is sought by the next of kin, the patient being dead, there must be legal identification of the next of kin. However personal records can be made available, without the permission of the patient under the following circumstances:

1. When referring the case to another doctor.
2. When demanded by the judiciary. The court requires the original record, and so when it is given, an attested copy should be made and retained by the MRD. Incidentally, information regarding alcohol and drug abuse can only be given to the court, and not to another party.
3. When requisitioned by the police. A written requisition must be insisted upon.
4. When asked for by insurance companies. The Insurance Act authorizes the Insurance Companies

to get this information, and the patient's consent is already given by the patient, when he signs the insurance contract.

5. When required for workman's compensation cases.
6. To defend the Doctor and the Hospital in malpractice suits.
7. When asked for by the Income Tax Authorities. This is provided in the Income Tax Act.
8. The HIV Status can only be given to the patient and not to any other. There has been debate as to the position of Public Health Authorities, in this regard, but it is better to err on the safer side, and ask for a court order.
9. The rules prevalent in different states may vary.

Types of Records

Though there are a number of types of Medical records at present, the Unit Record System is the preferred choice. In this system, each patient has only one case sheet or file, and is given a unique number as long as the patient continues to attend the hospital. This unique number is not allotted to any other patient. All the hospital data of the patient, irrespective of whether it is OP, IP, or Emergency are recorded in this file. It has the total and complete picture of the patient's history, therapy and investigations, excluding the necessity of referring to any other record, and its advantages are obvious. The disadvantage is that it can become bulky, and because it is taken out and assessed frequently, the outer cover can be damaged. This aspect can be remedied by practical adjustment, like using a thick cover, and replacing a damaged cover. This system is the most preferred system.

Format

By this we mean the method used in recording data in the patient's file. There are three types of format used:

Source Orientated

In this there are separate sections for doctors, nurses, lab, and accounts and so on. Most hospitals now use it, as it is simple and the staff is familiar with it. The different providers can access their portion directly, for example the nurse can go to the nursing section and see the earlier notes at one glance. But the disadvantage is that it does not give the total picture, and for this we have to refer to various sections. However most Indian Hospitals adopt this format, as it is more tidy and the doctors and nurses seem to prefer it.

Problem Orientated

This is said to be the better format, and many experts advocate it. In this the treating doctor has to identify each clinical problem separately, prioritize it and give it numbers like 1, 2, and so on. It has database, problem list, initial plan and problem notes. The advantage is that it lists all problems so that none are overlooked and each is addressed methodically. The disadvantage is that it is quite complex, and doctors have to be trained in its adoption.

Integrated Medical Records

Patient notes is recorded in a chronological order, meaning it has no separate sections for doctors, nurses etc, and the notes is written in the order the patient is seen. If the lab tests were done first, there are lab notes first, and if the nurse saw the patient after that, nurse's notes is given after the lab notes, and the doctor who saw the patient as the third person, writes his notes after the nurse's notes. The problem is that the data cannot be compared easily. For example if the nurse has to compare the temperature recorded earlier, and the present patient temperature, she has to wade through quite a number of notes. Moreover the notes have a jumbled look and most of the hospitals have given up this format.

Good Medical Record

It is now accepted that a good medical record is proof of good patient care. So the ingredients of the medical record assume importance. Many of these ingredients are summarized as under:

1. Legibility. Scrawling, scribbling, and use of unauthorized abbreviations are not acceptable.
2. Personal and clinical data must be completed. The personal data has to be written on all pages, and not confined to the first page.
3. The notes must be signed with name. Signature stamps may be accepted.
4. Date and time when entries were made must be written.
5. Mistakes should be scored out and not overwritten.
6. The format must be as per the laid down method.

The problem of incomplete records is of perpetual concern and has invited adverse comments from the judiciary. A senior busy doctor may skip the "paper work", but it will never be accepted as an excuse, resulting from serious consequences. An efficient method is for a medical record technician, to divide records as complete and incomplete, before filing, and the incomplete records will have to be completed by the person concerned within 24 hours.

Arrangement in the File

Hospitals have various methods of arranging, the case sheets and forms in the file. Some hospitals have separate files for OP and IP episodes, which are merged in the main file at the time of discharge. But whatever the method, the laid down order of arrangement has to be adhered to. The consensus is in favor of the following arrangement:

1. OP Records. Contains personal identification, personal data, clinical notes, lab tests ordered as OP and its results, and treatment prescribed as OP.
2. Correspondence. Contains referral letters, admission forms, consent forms, preoperative check up, medico-legal forms, birth notification and death reports.
3. Investigations. Lab reports, x-rays with x-ray report, other scans, ECG reports, etc all properly mounted.
4. In Patient Record. History, physical examination, doctors orders, progress notes, nurses notes, TPR charts, BP charts, procedure chart, pre-anesthesia check up, anesthesia chart, operation records, consent form, labor room record, diabetes chart, input/output chart, and discharge summary.

Divisions of MRD

The MRD is divided into separate divisions as under:

1. Reception
2. Medical records library
3. Statistics Section.

Reception

It is the central registry located at the registration counter of the OP, and controlled by the OP. All patients are registered here, and given a hospital number, which is unique for that patient and never allotted to another. The patient carries this number as long as he attends the hospital, even if he visits the hospital after years. A case chart is also initiated at this time. Though many types of allotting hospital numbers have been tried out, the best way is to have a common registration register, running serially for all patients including those who are consulting GPs, irrespective of specialties. Some advocate affixing a suffix to the number, to identify the specialty, example M for Medicine. The main function in this regard of the MRD is control of hospital numbers, and preparation of folders for later use.

Medical Records Library

Works round the clock, processing *both* OP and IP records. After OP hours the charts of those not admitted are sent to the MRD library, checked for completion and then filed. The records of discharged patients must be sent to the MRD, within 48 hours of discharge.

Statistics Section

Generates statistics and sends the birth reports.

Details of MRD

Space

A minimum of 100 sq m is required for hospitals up to 100 beds. For hospitals above 100 beds, an additional one sq m for each additional bed is required.

Equipment

Five to six shelved open ended steel racks, are still the preferred choice. Chairs, tables, working tables for sorting out case charts before filing, computers etc are the other requirement.

Staff

A Medical Records Officer (MRO), who has a recognized qualification in Medical Records, heads the MRD of medium and large hospitals. He reports directly to the Medical Director or Medical Superintend. The Medical Records Librarian and Medical Transcriptionist are the other staff.

Filing

The three usual method of filing used for medical records is as under:

Straight Numerical Filing

The filing is done in chronological order, as per OP number. It is easy to train filing clerks in this system, and weeding out is easier, as the earlier numbers relate to older files. But misfiling is more common as all digits are considered together.

Terminal Digital Filing

The hospital number, which is a six digital number, is divided into three, two digit components. The files are at first arranged as per the two last digits. Then they are rearranged as per the middle two digits, and lastly by the first two digits. In this system misfiling is less, but training of filing clerks is more difficult. As the cardinal aim is to minimize misfiling, this method is preferred.

Middle Digit Filing

No particular advantage and so it has been given up.

Weeding Out of Files

Because of the increased proliferation of files and as its bulk increases after each visit by the patient, the "paper octopus" is swallowing up hospital space. So periodical weeding out of files is an absolute necessity. But there is no official orders as to how long medical records must be kept, after which they can be destroyed. So each hospital is required to stipulate how long their records have to be kept, before they are destroyed, leading to wide variations. Our studies have been able to arrive at a reasonable and rational time stipulation for which the medical records must be retained, and then weeded out. This is as under:

- ☆ OP records: 5 years
- ☆ IP Records: 10 years
- ☆ Medico legal records: 20 years.

However it must be noted that it may differ from state to state.

The most important point to remember is that the period stipulated is not from the origin of the record, but from the date it was last accessed. Even then when a medical record is destroyed, a synopsis of these cases including personal details, admission and discharge dates, diagnosis, operation and labor room details, pathology reports, birth and death report etc has to be maintained.

Medical Transcription

This is not to be confused with the transcription of voice files, received from abroad, transcribed and then transmitted back through the inter net. The transcription, as far as MRD is concerned, is transcribing the written medical records in the Medical Record Library into a external memory like a CD or magnetic disc, in order to preserve it. The method of scanning and micro filming is costlier and more complex.

Computerization

The level of use of computer varies from hospital to hospital, depending upon the finance available and the computer culture present. But the belief that computerization is the answer to all evils is misplaced. It is NOT. When introducing, or extending computer services in MRD, the following questions must be answered:

1. How are the doctors or nurses clinical notes going to be entered?
2. What should be stored?
3. Where should it be stored?
4. How will it be accessed?
5. Security of stored data.

The MRD must have the following modules in its computer program:

1. *Registration Module*: Used to enter the personal details of the Patient, like name, age, sex, address, next of kin and his address, and telephone number of contacts. In response the computer must

generate a unique hospital number of six digits, and print an adhesive label, capable of being attached to the record. Access to the patient must be by name or address or Hospital number.

2. *Record Tracking Module*: Used to track charts issued out of MRD.
3. *Admission and Discharge Module*: Keeps track of admissions, and provides an IP number. It must have provision to indicate when patients are transferred to another ward, or to another room.
4. *Appointment Module*: Indicates the appointments given, and blocks appointments on holidays, or for a given period. It must indicate slots and time blocks, for giving appointments.

Missing Files

This problem produces the loudest noise in any hospital, and is referred to as the "missing file syndrome". Almost all missing files are due to misfiling, or the file being issued out to other departments and not being returned. The record tracking module in the MRD computer will be a great help in this regard. Clinicians also are helpless in proceeding with the management of a case without the previous records, and so insist on it. The missing file may be traced later, but the problem is how to deal with the angry patient now. The only practical solution is to make a new file, go to the clinician and explain the position to him, get the patient treated, and later merge this new file with the old one. This must be dealt with by the MRO himself.

Medical Audit

The most powerful tool available to measure the quality

of medical care provided. But this is resented by the clinicians at least in the beginning. Medical Records is the foundation of Medical Audit. The audit is done by the Medical Audit Committee, headed by the Medical Director or the Medical Superintend and the MRO is its secretary. Medical audit can be done internally (Internal Audit), or externally (External Audit).

Internal Audit

This is carried out by the MRD. All medical records of discharged patients, or who have died in the hospital for a stipulated period is collected and arranged date wise. Then the deficiencies in each record are indicated in a deficiency slip. The deficiencies are remedied in the conference room of the MRD. Here the professional aspect of medical care is not discussed, as it is a sensitive issue. There will be very little controversy in this kind of audit.

External Audit

Here other professionals evaluate the work of the treating team. The usual method is for the Medical Director or Medical Superintend, with a team of clinicians, to hold monthly meetings to discuss death cases, cases which do not show anticipated clinical progress, or interesting cases. This is attended by the MRO, the Nursing Superintend, and the head of the paramedical services. Alternatively an audit committee can be selected. The cardinal principle in external audit is not to go for "witch hunting", but to have a critical view of the case.

Chapter 8
Hospital Dietary Services

Diet is very much a part of medical treatment, and in diseases like Diabetes Mellitus it assumes a paramount role in management. The dietician is an important part of the clinical team and helps in producing the optimum clinical result. Moreover conditions like Obesity are the precursor of many human disability and disease, and diet plays a paramount and vital role in controlling obesity. It is in this context that it is a pity that the hospital dietary services are not given its due importance.

The object of the hospital dietary services is to provide appropriate, nourishing, appetizing and wholesome food to the patient. The service does this by selection of the food, purchasing it, storing it in optimum conditions, preparing it in the best way and distributing it in the most hygienic and attractive way.

Location

The preferred location of the dietary services and its main component the kitchen is the ground floor, taking the wind direction into account. It must be located in such a way that it is easy to deliver the raw supplies to it, and as close to the wards as possible. It should be large enough for an orderly method of food preparation and should be well ventilated.

Space

It will depend upon the bed strength of the hospital. The space required will also depend on whether the dietary is also providing canteen services to its employees. As ready reckoner small hospitals less than 100 beds require 8.9sq m (95 sq ft), a medium hospital from 100 to 250 beds will require 12.56 sq m (135 sq ft), and large hospitals above 250 beds will require 21.86 sq m (235 sq ft). This space is for patients only and if the dietary caters for employees also, a reasonable increase in space is required.

Organization

All large hospitals should have a qualified dietician. Every hospital must have two cooks, and two helpers, with separate staff providing the job of billing and collection of cash. The supervisor or in charge should report to the administrator or the medical superintend/medical director.

The kitchen staff must be trained in diet calculation, demand calculation, placing order to suppliers, checking items for quality, and proper storage. All food handlers must be trained in personal hygiene, and be medically examined once in a month. The record of these examinations, including stool examination must be displayed.

Kitchen staff is usually required to work for 14 hours, in two shifts.

Storage

Items should be stored so that there is no deterioration in quality. The kitchen should be daily inspected, for cleanliness and hygiene. Glasses and tumblers should be steam sterilized, by using perforated sheets over container with boiling water. As far as possible, cooked food should not be kept overnight. Perishable items like milk, butter and vegetables should be kept in Frigidaire or deep freezer. It must be remembered that hospital canteens are subject to being inspected by the state government health authorities.

Equipment

Purchases and contract for maintenance of kitchen equipment should preferably be through stores department. The kitchen equipment should be of good quality. A list of kitchen equipment required and their Indian BIS standards are given below for easy reference:

Equipment	*BIS Standard*
Bowl wash	IS:3994-1980
Steel chairs office type	IS:3499-1979 (Part 1)
Cooking Range with Oven	IS:4760-1979
Deep Fat Fryer	IS:10263-1982
Potato Peeler	
Gas Burners (Domestic Type)	IS::4246-1984
Kitchen Knives	IS:3546-1966

Equipment	*BIS Standard*
Refrigerator	
Deep Freezer	
Trolley for Hot Food	IS:10264-1982
Clock	
Cans 10 liters	
Rack for Utensils	
Sinks with work top	
Stainless spoons	
Strainers	
Table with marble top	
Steel chairs office type	
Dining tables	
Dining chairs	
Table office type	
Tumblers	
Table ware	
Table cloth	
Towels	
Food trays	IS:3256-1980
Weighing machine	IS:1853-1961

Chapter 9
Laundry Services

The aim of the Hospital Laundry is to provide clean, adequate, and timely supply of linen to the user departments. Hospital linen is usually composed of body and bed linen, as well as variety of clothing used for patient care. In this context Mechanical laundries in medium and large hospitals have become the preferred choice. Used linen from wards, delivery suites and Operation Theaters maybe infected, and so needs to be handled in a separate place.

Linen and Laundry service is an integral part of the hospital. Frequent change of linen, and washing of used linen, is an important factor in prevention of disease. Moreover clean and well pressed linen makes the hospital look more attractive. The adequacy of hospital Laundry Service will depend on the following:

- ☆ Provision of adequate linen, and its timely supply.

- Keeping a stock of clean washed linen.
- Laying down standing operation procedures (SOP), in collecting, cleaning and supplying linen.
- Cost effectiveness.

Types of Linen

A Hospital Laundry deals with the following types of linen:

- Bed linen-patients.
- Body linen-patients
- Operation Theater linen
- Labor Suite linen.
- Staff linen-uniforms, aprons, towels etc.
- Contaminated or infected linen
- Other types-like curtains, table clothes etc.

On an average about 5 kg of linen is generated per bed. Each patient gives every day or on alternate days, one towel, one pillow case, and two bed sheets. If patients are provided in-patient clothing, the patient also provides a pajama and jacket for male patients and a maxi for female patients. Additional linen will be from OT, Labor Room, Dressing Rooms and Maternity Wards. Blankets are washed by soap once in three months or as required, if soiled. At the collecting point the linen must be separated into soiled by use, items that are fowled by infective material, as well as staff uniforms, and then dealt with separately. While used linen and staff uniforms are washed by the normal method, contaminated items are collected in polythene bags, and goes through a process of sluicing, overnight soakage in disinfectant solution, before being washed in the routine manner. Baby linen is always considered contaminated. If the washing is by a contractor, contaminated clothing must be processed as above, in the hospital itself before being sent for washing. With introduction of Nuclear Medicine, and use of investigative procedures using isotopes, the question of dealing with linen which may be radio active, may require consideration. Such linen must be segregated and checked with a suitable radiation detector. The articles are then put through a special washer, meant for radio active linen, and when found free of any radiation activity, it is sent to the main laundry for routine washing.

Stocking of Linen

The point is that very few hospitals have 100 per cent occupancy. Moreover the frequency of routine bed linen change also plays a part. Daily change though ideal may be too expensive, but linen must be changed at least once in two days. After studies it is recommended that each occupied bed, must have five sets, one in use, one being washed,, one in transit, and two for weekends and holidays. A practical method of arriving at the number of occupied beds, for which linen must be provided is maximum daily occupancy, minus, average daily discharges, plus average daily admissions. Based on this the following norms per bed, should be stocked:

Bed Sheets (54"x90"), white or light colored	8
Draw sheets (7"x 90")	7
Patient towel	4
Woolen blanket (16"x25")	1 plus 20% extra.

Pillows	1 plus 20% extra
Pillow cover (one per each pillow)	4
Mattresses	1 plus 20% extra

Location and Space

Preferred choice is a separate building at a reasonable distance from the main building. It must have a minimum of four rooms as under.

Type	*No. of Hosp. Beds*	*No. of Rooms*	*Size in sq.m.*
Receiving Dirty Clothes	<100	One	0.93
	>100	One	1.12
Sorting/pre-cleaning	<100	One	1.03
	>100	One	1.68
Washing/drying/ironing	<100	One	2.60
	>100	One	3.90
Storing clean clothes	<100	One	0.93
	>100	One	1.20

Staffing

The laundry must be headed by a person who has experience in Laundry. It can be entrusted to a contractor. It is now believed that out sourcing of the laundry services is administratively more convenient. Supervision is preferably by the Nursing Superintend.

Equipment

Mechanical Laundry is preferable even for small

hospitals, as it is more methodical, time saving and cost effective. It reduces the risk of infection of the personnel handling the linen, and the suppliers must be responsible to train the persons, at the time of installation, and give refresher training periodically.

The nature of the power and water supply will determine the choice of the machine to be procured. By estimating the average load to be washed daily, and allowing for future increase, the size of the machine can be determined. It must be remembered that two half size machines are better than one big machine, since if one machine goes down, at least the other is available.

Functions

The main functions of a hospital laundry are as under:

- ☆ Collection of dirty linen from individual areas or departments.
- ☆ Transportation to central dirty collection point.
- ☆ Sorting linen into dirty or soiled, infected or foul, and linen soiled with blood or body fluids.
- ☆ Removal of blood stains and sluicing
- ☆ Disinfection or autoclaving.
- ☆ Washing and hydro extraction.
- ☆ Drying
- ☆ Repair of linen if required
- ☆ Pressing or Ironing
- ☆ Storage of clean linen
- ☆ Distribution to users
- ☆ Maintenance of record of Items received and distributed.

Care must be taken to separate the infected and non-infected linen. Foul linen should be handled as little as possible and such linen must be put in polythene bags and carefully secured, at its origin. Linen soiled with blood or body fluids must be transported in bags that prevent leakage.

Chapter 10
Hospital Mortuary

The mortuary is meant to receive and keep dead bodies. The bodies are kept in cold storage conditions to prevent the decay of the dead bodies, as decay is fast after death. In most hospitals, it will be under the control of the Casualty Medical Officer, while in teaching hospitals, it will be controlled by the head of the Forensic Medicine Department. The mortuary is responsible for conducting autopsies, medico legal autopsies only being carried out by hospitals so authorized. Trained Para medical staff is posted to the mortuary. Ethical considerations dictate that dead bodies must be dealt with in a dignified manner, and it must be accorded to all dead bodies. Any deficiency in the respect to be accorded to dead bodies, will evoke sentimental objections, and is likely to result in avoidable embarrassment.

Rules Regarding Mortuary Management

The rules would differ depending on the country where the hospital is located. However the general rules, with special reference to India is given below:

1. As a rule it should only receive bodies during Hospital hours. If in exceptional circumstances, it has to receive dead bodies after hospital hours, it has to be done, after getting permission of the hospital administrator.
2. The mortuary, normally receives bodies from the parent hospitals and associated hospitals if any. It also receives dead bodies sent by designated police stations. If it is required, in special circumstances to receive dead bodies from others, then it must get permission of the hospital administrator.
3. All bodies received by the mortuary must have identity tags securely tied to the body.
4. The request for keeping bodies must be accompanied by details regarding the Hospital or MLC (Medico Legal Case) number, the hospital ward, the name age, sex and the address of the dead person, duly signed by a authorized person, with his name and designation. If from another hospital it must be accompanied by a certificate stating that the death was a normal one, and that the dead person was not suffering from any infectious disease. In cases of medico legal implications, only the police can make the request for keeping the body in the mortuary.

5. The mortuary technician can only hand over non-MLC cases, and that too after proper identification, and after obtaining a receipt.
6. MLC cases can only be handed over to the police, after receiving a receipt giving the badge number, name and designation of the policeman.
7. Dead bodies cannot be kept in the mortuary for more than 72 hours.

Orders Regarding Autopsies

- ☆ Medico Legal Post-mortems are ordered after police investigation and inquest by the Coroner. Such autopsies are done by the Police Surgeon, or a specialist in Forensic medicine. Clinical post mortem can be done in hospitals, and it should be done by a Pathologist, after getting the permission of the next of kin.
- ☆ Autopsy should be done under normal light and not under artificial light.
- ☆ No unauthorized person should be allowed into the area where autopsy is being done.
- ☆ Dead bodies after a medico legal postmortem can only be handed over to the investigating police officer.
- ☆ After a clinical Post-mortem, the body can be handed over to the next of kin after obtaining a receipt.
- ☆ Post-mortems should be done before six pm, and never after sunset
- ☆ The autopsy reports must be written at the place of the post-mortem, and not in another place later.

Carrying out post-mortems is a sensitive issue and liable to raise many controversies. The post-mortem has to be completed, and all relevant parts must be examined. It must be done before sunset and the report must be written as the post-mortem proceeds and at the place where he post-mortem has been done. The usual legal mistake is that the findings are not recorded as the post-mortem is done, but later.

Chapter 11
Transport

Hospital transport can broadly be divided into three, the Ambulance, General Transport, and Patient moving devices.

Ambulance

The common mistake is to conceive the Ambulance, as a vehicle to transport patients, and sometimes hospital staff when other vehicles are not readily available. But the ambulance is meant not only to transport a patient, but to render medical care during transportation, and to cope with emergencies outside the hospital. The Ambulance has two compartments, one for the driver and the other for the patient. It must carry equipment and supplies, to ensure optimum medical care at the site, and during transportation, till the patient reaches the hospital casualty. The arrangements available in the Ambulance must ensure that the patient's condition is not aggravated during transportation, and maximum safety and comfort is available during this period. The purpose of the ambulance can be summarized as under:

- ☆ Accident and Emergency services
- ☆ Patient transportation service, with medical care during transport.
- ☆ It is not to be used for transportation of hospital staff.
- ☆ Though it is not to be used for transporting dead bodies, practice seems to have sanctioned this.

Accident and Emergency services, available in the Ambulance must be capable of responding to calls round the clock, and providing quick and adequate response, to life threatening situations. There must be a system to monitor the response time of the ambulances, so that bottlenecks can be removed. Doctors especially Casualty Medical Officers, nurses and paramedical personnel may have to accompany the ambulances, and they must have adequate training in emergency medical care and resuscitation. They also must have a high level of clinical skills to deal with heart attacks, or severe trauma with shock.

Equipment

The equipment and medical supplies available in an ambulance must be capable of dealing with life threatening situations, and resuscitate the patient. Unfortunately most of the ambulance providers are ignorant of this requirement, and so Ambulances are not provided such equipment. Therefore we think it necessary, to enumerate the minimum equipment and drugs an ambulance must carry at all times. Ambulances must be subject to surprise checks in this regard, and harsh penalty must be imposed on Ambulances who transgress this order.

Essential Equipment

- ☆ Portable suction apparatus.
- ☆ Hand operated bag for ventilating the patient (Ambu Bag).
- ☆ Airways of different sizes including infant sizes.
- ☆ Mouth gags.
- ☆ Resucitubes.
- ☆ Portable oxygen cylinder.
- ☆ Sterile intravenous equipment.
- ☆ Sterile universal dressing.
- ☆ Splints including Thomas Splint.
- ☆ Portable ECG equipment.
- ☆ Portable Defibrillator.
- ☆ Poison kit.
- ☆ Sterile Obstetrical equipment.
- ☆ BP apparatus.
- ☆ Stethoscopes.
- ☆ Blood glucose estimation equipment.
- ☆ Sterile syringes, needle.
- ☆ IV canulas (peripheral and external jugular)

Essential Drugs

- ☆ Adenosine.
- ☆ Adrenaline.

- Atropine.
- Betnesol.
- Dextrose–50 per cent, 25 per cent, 5 per cent.
- Dopamine.
- Frusemide.
- Glucagons.
- Haemaccel.
- Lignocaine.
- Metoclopramide.
- Midazolam.
- Morphine.
- Nalaxone.
- Salbutamol.
- Sodium Bicarbonate.
- Normal saline/Ringer lactate.

When stocking drugs, it must be periodically turned over to prevent life expired drugs being carried.

Legally Ambulances cannot be used for any other purpose other than for transporting patients.

General Transport

Consists of, cars, trucks and motor cycles. Its management is the same as in other institutions.

Moving Devices for Patients

Consists of patient trolleys, and wheel chairs, Bays are provided for them, mainly at the entry of OPD, Casualty, Labor Suite, OT, and wards. The main point which should be considered in this context is maintenance of this equipment. They must be oiled and checked every week as per a laid down schedule. The patient trolley making a racket as it moves along the corridors, reflects badly on the image of a good hospital. Patient trolleys and wheel chairs must be available at the places where they will be required, and staff should not be made to go searching for it, making the patients wait, and leaving the relatives fuming. The other point is that as far as possible the patient trolleys and wheel chairs must be pushed by the hospital staff, and the relatives must not be asked to handle them.

Chapter 12

Fire Prevention

With this chapter we begin the Hospital Supporting Systems.

Break out of fire anywhere, is a disaster. But in hospitals, with helpless patients, pregnant mothers and newly born infants, the break out of fire is a tragedy of unimaginable proportions. The greater tragedy is that, most of these fires can be prevented. Even when it occurs the consequences, to a large extent is minimized, if there is a fire prevention drill in the hospital, which has been practiced periodically. Therefore Fire Protection Program has to be an important part of the general safety program of each and every hospital.

The program begins with the building of the hospital. All functional units should have stairs as fire exits, in addition to lifts. The usual mistake is to clutter this stair case with unwanted material, effectively blocking them, making them useless in an emergency. These fire exit stairways, must be kept free between the different stories of the building, and must be inspected daily to ensure this.

It is true that the maintenance of hospital building and its safety, mainly rests with the engineering and electrical sections of the hospital, but the hospital administrator cannot absolve himself from supervision and scrutiny in this regard. All hospitals must constitute a hospital safety committee, including the engineering hospital component, and heads of high risk areas like O T, laboratory, store, medical records, kitchen etc. These high risk areas must have automatic fire alarms and separate fire extinguisher facilities. The usual facilities recommended are smoke detection alarms, heat activated alarms, automatic water sprinklers, and fire extinguishers. The multi storied hospitals must be provided with wide open areas all around, to facilitate entry of fire fighting personnel.

All hospitals have to obtain a certificate from the local fire prevention authorities, and adhere to the norms laid down by them. It must have close liaison with the nearest fire fighting station.

Medium and Large hospitals must have fire hydrants and electric pumps as well as a generator, to provide electricity to operate emergency lifts, and illuminate fire exits. Many hospital fires have been found to be due to electric short circuits, and so the electrical lines must be checked as per a laid down schedule, and a record must be maintained regarding this check.

All staff must be trained in fire fighting drill, and mock drills must be practiced frequently and a record kept. But the best option is to prevent fires. The important aspect of fore prevention in hospitals are:

- *Good House Keeping*: Elimination of all combustible material from the hospital. Special attention should be given to attics, basements, closets, and stores.
- *Good Maintenance*: All mechanical and electrical equipment must be monitored. Importance in maintenance of fire protection devices like fire alarm systems, portable fire extinguishers, and automatic water sprinklers.
- *Good Employee Discipline*: All staff must be aware of the fire prevention methods and must be trained in fire fighting drills.

The most important aspect of fire prevention is not providing the equipment alone. The fire fighting equipment must be periodically and methodically examined to ensure that it is functional. Fire drills must be conducted meticulously, and a record of the same must be maintained.

Chapter 13
Engineering

The engineering elements in a hospital can be broadly divided into Bio Medical Engineering and General Engineering. While Bio Medical job is a technical job carried out by a qualified engineer with a college degree in his specialty, general engineering in most hospitals is a "handy man's" job. Employing more qualified personnel in the section of general engineering of the hospital, requires serious and urgent consideration.

Bio Medical Engineering

There is ever increasing use of high technology based equipments, in hospitals. Because of this, bio medical engineering, as a separate science, has emerged. There is a four year degree course in Bio Medical Engineering in colleges. After passing out he is required to do an internship. In simple terms, Bio Medical Engineering is application of principles of engineering, in the medical field.

The usual pattern is to have a small workshop for bio medical engineering, and have two separate sections, one for minor equipment, and the other for major equipment. It is managed by a qualified bio medical engineer (B Tech). Apart from repair and maintenance of the equipment, he is responsible for keeping a history sheet for major equipment, and for entering into Annual Maintenance Contract (AMC). In the present context Bio Medical Engineering has become essential in most hospitals.

Engineering

Some describe a hospital as a ship at high sea. As exigencies have to be attended by the ship on the spot, so also, most exigencies in a hospital have to be attended immediately, and on the spot. These services will include plumbers, electricians, lift operators etc. The most important function would be preventive maintenance. If preventive maintenance is done methodically, many of the patient's complaints can be avoided. In a hospital, it involves calculation of the usual time equipment will function efficiently, and replacement accordingly. Waiting for the equipment to fail, is bad practice.

The plumber and electrician must do daily rounds of the hospital, correcting small deficiencies on the spot. The departments especially the wards must also keep a note book in which complaints are recorded with time, and reported to the concerned tradesman. The time it was rectified also must be entered. The most irritating thing for a patient is to have his toilet not working, and when he complains that it is still not working, for the nurse to tell him it has been reported! Please remember it is these small things which blow up into a crisis.

Maintenance of the Buildings

A senior person preferably from the engineering section must be made responsible to maintain hospital buildings. He must prepare a time schedule for this maintenance. He must make arrangements to attend to emergencies, including water supply and sewerage. He must have authority to carry out minor repairs. He must supervise minor and major repair works.

Horticulture

The person entrusted with the job of maintaining the buildings can also be entrusted with the horticulture of the hospital grounds. A master plan to develop the hospital horticulture surroundings should be prepared in consultation with others, and executed in phases. Maintenance of lawns, flower beds and trees, has to be done with the help of gardeners.

Chapter 14

Security Section

As you enter a hospital in India, the first person you see is the security man standing at the entrance. The security man can be an asset to the hospital if he is good and knows his job or a liability if he is shabby and uncouth. The truth of the proverb "the first impression is the best impression" is born out by the hospital security. The main problem is that we employ any one as security, the selection being limited, as it is considered an unskilled job. The hospital does not tell him what to do, only expecting him to salute the Boss as he comes in, and do not even think of training him. After all this, we bemoan that "the Security in my hospital is so bad that it is beyond redemption".

The first thing to improve things is to give the security, dignity. You have to make him understand that he is a very important member of the hospital team, and other things will follow. He must be made aware of his duties, clearly and precisely.

He must follow certain standards:

- ☆ *Appearance*: He must be smartly dressed in the prescribed uniform. It must be clean and well pressed.
- ☆ *Posture*: A lazy posture or lounging is totally unacceptable. Standing with both his hands in his pockets is atrocious.
- ☆ *Courtesy*: He must invariably be polite, and show a willingness to help.
- ☆ *Knowledge*: He must be aware where the departments are, and which doctors are on leave. This will enable him to inform and assist the incoming patients.
- ☆ He must assist the elderly and the disabled to get down from the vehicle and navigate the entrance to the hospital.
- ☆ At the casualty he must help in unloading the patients.
- ☆ He must help in parking vehicles in the appropriate area but should not be officious about it.

The number of security persons required will differ from hospital to hospital, and is a matter of judgment. The in charge of security controls the activity of the security section, and he monitors the activity of the security personnel.

His main duty is to ensure that unauthorized persons do not enter the hospital. As his name suggests he is responsible for the security of the hospital especially after office hours. He is required to regulate the traffic and ensure that the entrance and exit to the hospital is not clogged or obstructed. He must be told that minutes wasted in either entering a hospital, or an emergency being taken out of the hospital, may result in the loss of a precious life.

He has a heavy responsibility in regulating visitors outside visiting hours. It is here he has to be firm as well as polite and considerate. Considerable disturbance can arise as visitors insist that it is their right to visit their relatives admitted to the hospital, and is not prepared to listen to the inconvenience caused by them not sticking to the visiting hours. The fact that they know that they are wrong in transgressing the laid down visiting hours, only makes them more aggressive and rude, especially if they are people who have a high notion of their own importance. Here the skill in diplomacy of the Security person will be severely tested. Another area is when the Security person insists on a gate pass for taking out items and equipment outside the hospital. Here again the self proclaimed leaders among the hospital staff, who flaunt their importance can produce unpleasant situations.

To sum up, the security personnel play an important part in projecting the image of the hospital. He is worth his weight in gold.

Chapter 15

Public Relations

A hospital is part of a social system. Firstly it has to deal with professionals like doctors, nurses, medical technicians and other paramedical personnel. Secondly it has to deal with personnel who are part of the management services, like dietary, laundry, supplies, house-keeping, accounts, security and so on. Thirdly it has to deal with patients, their relatives, visitors, and the community at large. So, the hospital has to more than satisfy its actual customers. Public relations, therefore is the promotion of a positive image of the hospital. It is a combination of:

- ☆ Impression of the users and the public.
- ☆ Attitude of the people working for the hospital.
- ☆ Attitude of the Hospital Administration.

The needs of each of the above categories differ. Patients want effective services and a sympathetic approach.

Workers (staff) want job satisfaction, and recognition. Hospital administration wants efficiency, financial viability, and maximum satisfaction of patients and staff.

Basis of Public Relations

The patient, his relatives and family, are a bundle of expectations, anxieties, hopes and fears. They are not very interested in the number of beds and specialties, and seek satisfaction of their physical, psychological and emotional needs. His prime need, when not critically ill, is for privacy. He requires to be informed about his illness, and his clinical progress. He needs freedom from pain, and the assurance that he will be looked after, in time of crisis. He needs to have confidence in the people caring for him. Even with government providing the finances, as in government hospitals, it can only fulfill its role, by maintaining the confidence of the community it serves. The public is becoming more and more conscious of its rights and privileges. It is seen that the patient's dissatisfaction is often not against the medical care given, but pertains to the bed, food and other services provided. This highlights the importance of each member of the hospital in promoting the good image of the hospital. One of the most irritating patterns in a hospital is entry of a number of health professionals, into the patients' territory, even without knocking or announcing, examining without telling the patient the reason for the examination, and then abruptly leaving without an explanation for the professional activities. Many times you get the impression, that the patient is treated as the trespasser, and not the hospital staff. Good publicity by itself is not good public relations, though it is very much a part of public relations.

Basis of Good Image

The three important things that project a positive image of the hospital are:

1. Technically competent medical care.
2. Mutual trust and courtesy between the hospital and its clients. The term client includes the patient, his relatives and visitors.
3. Goodwill and understanding between the hospital staff.

The problem is that public relations cannot be measured quantitatively. But the extent of this can be gathered by asking the patients and their relatives, their general impression about a particular hospital. Creation of a good impression cannot be left to chance, but it has to be carefully created, and this is where public relations come in. The most important point is the manner the hospital patient care activities are carried out. We have to treat a patient as an individual, not leaving his body specially the private parts exposed, minimizing bodily contact, providing explanation why procedures are being done, and recognizing the physical as well as the psychological discomfort, that arise from invasion of privacy. The usual complaints are:

- ☆ Indifferent care and lack of human touch.
- ☆ Low quality of care as assessed by the patient, by the quality of linen, diet, equipment, facilities, cleanliness etc.
- ☆ Lack of guidance including sign posting, oral directions etc.

- ☆ Lack of information especially about his disease condition.
- ☆ Lack of comforts, like chairs, benches, drinking water, toilets etc.
- ☆ Delays in each step, including billing.
- ☆ Overcrowding.
- ☆ Long ques.
- ☆ Noise.
- ☆ Poor sanitation.
- ☆ Behavior of staff.

Methods of Promoting Good Public Relations

These can be divided into two, namely the Operative method and the Communicative method.

Operative Method

All staff of the hospital is involved, including telephone operators, enquiry personnel, admission office clerks, accountants etc. The ingredients of this method are cheerful and courteous behavior, prompt and efficient service, as well as the well kept appearance of the staff. Please remember that to make others happy, you must be happy yourself, and so worker morale assumes importance. The areas requiring special attention are OPDs, especially high waiting time; delay in getting lab results, delay at the pharmacy, etc. The other aspect is cleanliness, courteous behavior towards visitors, and serving of hot appetizing food. Availability of Medical social workers and Community Health Workers are a great help.

Communicative Methods

In this method, we employ all methods of communication. Those include making available appropriate information to patients, an open house approach to visitors, accepting the fact that a large number of visitors is unavoidable in the social setting of developing countries, availability of a senior nurse to answer questions during the visiting time by the patient's relatives, administrative rounds, provision of a complaint box, a hospital brochure, visits by social groups, holding of annual day, talks and interviews on TV etc.

Public Relations Officer (PRO)

There must be an officer for doing public relations work. He must have a flair and aptitude in public relations. His duties are-

1. Establishing contact with the public media.
2. On a particular day, preferably the hospital day, he must invite correspondents of the print, TV and electronic media, social workers as well as selected political leaders, take them round the hospital, briefing them about the hospital.
3. He will be the spokes person of the hospital.
4. In time of strikes he will organize the hospital functioning so that the patient care is not interrupted.
5. His office will be in the complex where the casualty is located.
6. He will establish good relations between the hospital and the community. He will convey the

important events regarding the success of the hospital to the media.

Indicators for Measuring Public Relations

- ☆ Patient satisfaction surveys.
- ☆ General opinion poll.
- ☆ Number of complaints received.
- ☆ Turn over of medical staff.
- ☆ Consistency in patient's attendance.
- ☆ Inpatients leaving against medical advice.
- ☆ Letters to the editor in the local press.

Additional Considerations: An understanding and supportive press and media can be a great help in public relations. If things go wrong, a quick press conference may help. All information concerning a patient, must be given only with the consent of the patient, after clearance by the public relations. Good nursing staff is a great asset in this regard. If there is a local women's organization, their help should be sought.

Chapter 16
Marketing

In this chapter, we will be dealing with an important aspect of hospital functioning namely marketing. Both marketing and public relations aim at projecting a positive image of the hospital. Creating a positive image is not by chance alone, but has to be planned, and actuated by conscious effort. Providing a high quality service is not fully adequate, but the public has to be educated on the problems and limitations of the hospital.

Earlier when I passed out and joined a hospital in 1950, advertising was synonymous with canvassing, and was a bad word, in the context of the hospital care system. It was our belief, held as sacrosanct, that all we had to was to create a good hospital and staff it with capable health professionals, that is doctor, nurses and paramedical staff. Once this was done, the patients would come automatically.

But now the hospital marketing has come of age. The entry of corporate hospitals, coupled with the awareness regarding medical tourism, with India becoming a sought after destination for medical tourism, has radically changed the situation. Gone are the days when hospitals, could depend upon, mere word of mouth promotion to attract patients. It is now accepted, that marketing is a useful function in hospital planning and activities. Promotion including marketing of hospital, is no more considered as inherently bad, but is viewed as an important communication activity. The word "customer", in a hospital context, is no more a bad word.

The other factor is that medical tourism has become an important factor in earning foreign exchange. But we in India have not fully developed the mechanism to attract foreign visitors, wanting medical services. This is in spite of the fact, that we have world class hospital facilities and service, at costs far below international rates. Out of all the services we can offer to a foreigner, medical services are one of the most attractive. India requires to aggressively sell medical services abroad.

The increasing trend for health insurance has made price competition, an important marketing tool. We will have premium incentives, new attitudes to admissions and discharges, improved food services, "package pricing" etc. In this context, hospitals have to be more receptive to new marketing philosophy, and new marketing strategies.

The emerging alternative is a competitive health care industry, with carefully devised marketing strategies, for newer market productions.

Differing Views on Hospital Marketing

Some of the differing views expressed on hospital marketing is given below:

- ☆ Patients are the best ambassadors for a hospital, and so the focus should be on meeting their needs. Their fears and anxieties should be addressed, and every satisfied customer, will bring in many more.
- ☆ We can no more rely on word of mouth promotion, for getting patients. Hospitals have to become more aggressive, to survive the fierce competition.
- ☆ Aggressive marketing is not necessary in hospital care sector, as it is not likely to bring in more patients. Patients choose a hospital, based on facilities available, expertise of the doctors and their reputation, and its nearness to their residence.
- ☆ Hospital marketing has to change from the subtle to the aggressive.
- ☆ Tertiary care hospitals will have to do research on different segments, to identify the segments from which the patients are not turning up. For example if market research shows that a hospital is not attracting patients above the age of 60, the focus should be on this group, and geriatric medicine.

But in today's context, there has to be a change in the concept of hospital marketing.

Hospital Marketing Concept

Basically it is the same as in a service industry, one section provides service and the others consume it. Marketing is interplay between the providers and the consumer. But in hospital services, we are marketing intangibles, not subject to strict quantitative end results, and so marketing becomes more complex. Moreover many times, the doctor, who is the provider, is also the marketer.

With the acceptance of marketing as an important hospital activity, the necessity of a marketing department in a hospital has been acknowledged. As the investment in a modern hospital is substantial, it stands to reason, that selling hospital services require a proper system. As far as medical tourism is concerned, the marketing department establishes liaisons with the doctors of the foreign countries, creating an awareness of the facilities available, and its cost.

Marketing Strategies

Continuous medical education, namely awareness clinics in OPD, medical camps, check up programs for executives, specialists appearing on visual media and celebrating yearly days for certain diseases, are some of them. But the most innovative is "marketing as war".

Marketing Viewed as War

This is my favorite, naturally because I have served as a doctor in the Defence Forces, for 33 years, retiring in 1985, in the rank of a Brigadier. Marketing in simple words, is an activity directed at satisfying needs, through an exchange process. Most of the market strategy of our hospitals, in the past, is to do market research on the needs of the patient, and then devise methods to meet it. It is based on the concept that the customer (patient) is king. But the weakness in this strategy is that all hospitals adopt this strategy, and so its adoption does not give us an edge. The new theory is that instead of hospital marketing being patient orientated, it should be competitor orientated. Our focus must be on our competitors. Today hospitals require to look closely at their competitors, identifying their weak points, and launching market attacks against these points. The efficacy of this strategy has been proved by the success stories of many companies. Digital Equipment Corporation made millions by exploiting the weakness of IBM in small computers; Savin established a successful break through in inexpensive copiers, a weak point in Xerox line up; Pepsi taking advantage of its sweet taste to upstage Coke, the stories go on.

In the plans for the future, much more attention will have to be paid by the hospitals to its competitors. Dossiers may have to be compiled on each of our competitor hospitals, their key marketing people and their style. This is similar to what generals of opposing armies do, during war, in regard to the enemy generals. The marketing people will have to wage a marketing war, and their plans will have to be modeled on military campaigns. They will have to learn how to attack, how to flank their competitors, how to defend their positions and when to adopt Guerilla tactics. This is the same technique, football teams' use, as they outwit, outflank, and outplay their opponents, the result being displayed as goals, on the score board. In war also, you win by outwitting, out flanking and overpowering you enemy, the territory you conquer being a reflection, on your ability to do these things. Marketing of hospitals is not too different. Please remember, that in war, you not only strive to win, but also not to lose.

History tells us that in the last 3500 years, after recorded history began, only in about 270 years, there has been no war. The weapons used in these wars, is no more used, but the principles of war, still remain valid to a large extent. Some of these principles like working in unison, concentration of force, operating on lines of least expectation, deploying forces in an overpowering mass, and so on, are valid in hospital marketing war also. While it is not possible or necessary to list all the wars from which these principles rose, a few are listed below, just as a matter of interest.

Marathon: 450 BC

15000 Persians, from the area now called Iran, landed at the bay of Marathon, north east of Athens, in Greece. The Greeks were numerically inferior, having only 11000 troops. But the Greeks had a big advantage, in their use of "phalynx". Each Greek soldier held his shield in such a way, that it overlapped that of his neighbor, protecting half of himself and half of the soldier on his left. This was more than a match to the numerically superior Persians, who were used to one to one combat. The result was stunning. 6000 Persians died against 200 of the Greek. The military principle of working in unison, and concentration of force was born, a principle valid even today.

Arbella: 331 BC

After victories on the Danube, Alexander the Great returned to find that Darius had mobilized a Greek army against him, by spreading the rumor that Alexander's army had perished. Darius did this through an agent called Demosthenes, probably the first advertising agent in history. A decisive confrontation took place at Arbella. Darius arranged his troops in the conventional way, with 15 elephants and 200 chariots in front. Alexander had Calvary (horsed soldiers), on both flanks, and he attacked the right flank of the enemy, with his Calvary. When Darius turned to meet this attack, Alexander wheeled his Calvary to the center, and broke through the enemy's front. This tactic used by Alexander was used for another 2000 years, and to some extent is still used in modern warfare. This is how the principle "successful armies operate on the line of least expectation" was born.

Metaurus: 207 BC

Carthaginian armies from Tripoli was ravaging Italy, led by two brothers, Hannibal in the south, and Hasdrubal in the north. The Carthaginians used elephants to lead their charges, the forerunner of tanks. But the brothers made the mistake of dividing their armies. The roman general Nero (not the emperor who played the violin when Rome burned), started to move to south towards Hannibal, but during the night he changed direction and moved north. This out flanking move brought the Romans a great victory. Modern military principle "keeping the forces concentrated in an overpowering mass" is still valid.

The precedence's are many and too long. The best strategy in hospital marketing today is to view marketing as war, and use the military principles of war, in its execution. Hospital marketing will have to give up the strategy of concentrating on the customer (patient), and focus on its competitors.

Chapter 17
Hospital Waste Disposal

Hospital Waste

Hospital waste is of many types. House keeping activity generates considerable amount of trash, and the visitors bring with them food and other materials, which have to be disposed off. In addition, hospitals generate pathological waste-blood soaked dressings, human anatomical parts, disposable items etc. These waste items have to be disposed off quickly lest they putrefy, emit foul smell and act as reservoirs of infection. In our hospitals the main problems are defective sewage, and incorrect waste disposal. Many of our hospitals in developing countries do not have a waste management and disposal policy. The junior most member of the house keeping team is entrusted with the job, without any supervision. Waste management is not given the importance that it deserves, and so hospitals only allot meager resc urces to this activity. A clean hospital and good house keeping, have a direct effect on health. Cleanliness radiates cheer, and a well kept hospital, inspires confidence.

"Waste" is any discarded or unwanted residual material arising from the hospital or activities related to the hospital. "Disposal" covers the total process of collecting, handling, packing, storage, transportation, and final disposal.

Volume

In waste disposal, volume of the waste disposed of, and its category, assumes importance. Studies in Indian cities indicate that the refuge or waste varied from 0.48 to 0.6 kg, per person, per day, and the matter which can be composted varying from 30 to 40 per cent. On an average, the volume of total solid waste, in Indian hospitals, vary between 1 kg to 3 kg per day per bed, of which 0.25 kg consists of food. The composition of this waste was found to be as under:

- Bandages, gauze, cotton waste: 34 per cent
- Coal ash: 31 per cent
- Foliage (leaves etc): 14 per cent
- Food waste: 11.5 per cent
- Trash: 5 per cent
- Biological waste: 2.5 per cent
- Glass bottles etc: 2 per cent
- Of these waste, 67 per cent originate from the wards (IP Area), 14.0 per cent from the OPD, and 19.0 per cent from the service areas.

Types of Hospital Waste

The type of hospital waste can broadly be classified into solid waste, and liquid waste.

Solid Waste

Includes the following:

- *Dry garbage*: Ordinary floor refuse, papers, flowers, trash.
- *Wet garbage*: Waste from kitchen (fruit, peels, left over food)
- *Wet tissues and bones*: (from operation theaters, labor room, mortuary, and laboratory).
- *Plaster casts*: From plaster room.
- *Packing materials*: Cardboard cartons, paper packets etc.
- *Biological waste*: Dressing, cotton pads,
- *Metal waste*: Tin cans, bottle caps, needles.
- *Glass*: Broken bottles, broken vials, and syringes.
- *Disposable plastic items*: Originates from all areas of hospitals.

Liquid Waste

It covers sullage and sewerage, which emanates from bathrooms, lavatory, toilets, kitchen, pantries, operation theaters, dressing rooms, laboratory, laundry and chemical developer fluid from the radiology department. The quantity of total liquid waste in India is estimated as 300 to 400 liters, per day, per bed.

A third group is from large or teaching hospitals, and is waste from radiotherapy, and nuclear medicine department. It is very little, but requires careful disposal.

Points Requiring Attention

- ☆ Every hospital must make all efforts to implement the Biomedical Waste (Management and Handling) Rules, notified under the relevant Environment Protection Act.
- ☆ Each hospital must take appropriate authorization from the competent authority, for the different activities connected with waste management.
- ☆ A hospital waste management committee, chaired by the head of the institute should be constituted, and this committee should lay down a specific action plan for waste management.
- ☆ The hospital must make all out effort, to prevent recycling of disposable items like syringes, needles, catheters etc.
- ☆ The reports and returns laid down to, must be complied with.
- ☆ In case waste needs to be transported outside the hospital for treatment, adequate precaution as laid down in the rules must be complied with.

Biomedical Waste

Disposal of this hazardous waste must be according to the laid down Biomedical waste (Management and Handling) rules.

Definition of Biomedical Waste

Biomedical waste means waste, which is generated during the diagnosis, treatment or immunization of human beings, or animals or in research activities pertaining thereto, or in the production or testing of biologicals.

Categories of Biomedical Waste

This waste must be segregated into the following categories. Certain categories require treatment before transportation.

- ☆ Category No. 1: Human Anatomical Waste-Human tissues, organs, body parts.
- ☆ Category No. 2: Animal Waste. Animal tissues, organs, body parts, carcasses, bleeding parts, fluid and blood of experimental animals used in research, waste from Vetinary hospitals, or animal houses.
- ☆ Category No.3: Microbiological and Biotechnology wastes. Waste from laboratories, cultures, stock or specimens of micro-organisms, live or attenuated vaccines, human and animal cell culture used in research, and infectious agents from research and industrial laboratories, waste from production of biologicals, toxins, dishes and devices used for transfer of cultures.
- ☆ Category No.4: Sharps. Needles, syringes, scalpels, blades, glass etc. which can cause puncture or cuts. This includes both used and unused items.
- ☆ Category No.5: Discarded Medicines and Cytotoxic waste. Contain time expired, contaminated and discarded medicines.
- ☆ Category No.6: Soiled waste. Items contaminated with blood and body fluids, including cotton, dressings, soiled plaster casts, linen, bedding, and others contaminated with blood.

- ☆ Category No. 7: Solid Waste. Waste generated from disposable items, other than sharps: like tubing, catheters, intravenous sets etc.
- ☆ Category No. 8: Liquid Waste. Waste generated from laboratory and washing, cleaning, housekeeping, and disinfecting agents.
- ☆ Category No. 9: Incinerator Waste. Ash, from incinerators.
- ☆ Category No.10: Chemical Wastes. Chemicals used in production of biologicals, chemicals used in disinfection, and insecticides.

Waste Segregation

It should be done at the source of generation, the usual areas being, all patient care areas, diagnostic service, operation theaters, labor rooms; treatment rooms etc. Responsibility for segregation is that of the generator, the nurse in charge or in charge of the departments. The biomedical wastes must be segregated as per the category under which it comes.

Biomedical Waste Collection

This is to be done as per the biomedical waste rules. However a separate container must be placed at every point of generation of general waste, as distinct from biomedical waste, and this general waste is to be collected by the municipality from a common collecting point. No infectious waste should be put into this container. The trolleys used to collect hospital waste, should be so designed so as to ensure that there is no spillage or leakage of biomedical waste, during transportation. The type of container, and color code for each category of biomedical waste has been specified.

Containers having different colored bags should be located at the point of generation. These bags should be filled only to 3/4th of its capacity, tied securely, labeled and removed from the site of generation, regularly. Certain categories of waste, which need disinfection or decontamination, at the site of generation, such as plastic and sharp material, should be removed, from the site of generation, only after treatment.

As a precaution against HIV infection, all material contaminated by blood or body fluids, must be soaked in 10 per cent bleaching powder solution, for 30 minutes, before being put into the collection colored bag. It is difficult to keep plastic bags standing by itself and so same colored buckets must be used. An estimate must be made for the amount and kind of plastic bags required for 3 months, so that bulk orders can be placed.

The categories, type of container and color coding is given in the succeeding table.

The important points to be remembered are:

- ☆ All the items sent to incineration/deep burial (categories 1,2,3, and 6) should be placed in yellow colored bags.
- ☆ All the biomedical waste to be sent for microwave/autoclave/chemical treatment should be placed in red colored bags.
- ☆ The plastic bags which contain liquid like blood, urine, pus etc should be put into red colored bag for microwaving/autoclaving, and other items

should be put into white or blue bag, after chemical treatment, for destruction or shredding.

The Category of the waste, type of container and color coding is given below in a tabular form.

Category	*Type of Container*	*Color Coding*
Human anatomical waste	Plastic bag	Yellow
Animal waste	Plastic bag	Yellow
Microbiological and Biotechnology waste	Plastic bag	Yellow
Sharps	Plastic bag, puncture proof and translucent	Blue/White
Discarded medicine and cytoxic waste	Plastic bag	Black
Soiled solid waste	Plastic bag	Yellow/Red
Solid waste	Plastic bag, translucent	Blue/White
Liquid waste	Plastic bag	Red
Incineration ash	Plastic bag	Black
Chemical waste (solid)	Plastic bag	Black

Storage of Waste

Storage refers to holding of biomedical waste for certain period of time, after which it is sent for treatment and disposal. It is the duration of time, for which the waste is kept at the site of generation, before transit to the point of treatment and disposal. The cardinal rule is "No untreated biomedical waste shall be kept or stored beyond 48 hours".

- ✩ If it becomes necessary to keep it beyond 48 hours, the permission of the prescribed authority must be obtained.

- When kept beyond 48 hours, it must be ensured by the authorized person that it does not adversely affect human health or environment.

Transportation

Transportation will consist of transport inside the hospital, and transport outside the hospital.

Inside the Hospital

- Within the hospital, waste routes must be designated, to avoid passage of waste through patient care areas.
- Separate time must be designated for transport of biomedical waste, so as to reduce the risk of it, getting mixed with general waste.
- Dedicated wheeled containers, trolleys or carts should be used to transport waste bins or bags, to the site of storage or treatment.
- Trolleys and carts should be thoroughly cleaned, and disinfected in the event of any spillage.
- The wheeled containers must be designed in such a way, that the waste can easily be loaded, remains secured during transportation, does not have any sharp edges and the container is easy to clean and disinfect.

Outside the Hospital

- Untreated biomedical waste shall be transported, only by authorized vehicles, so authorized by the competent authority, as specified by the government under the Motor Vehicles Act.

- The contents for transportation must be labeled as given in Schedule III and IV of the Biomedical Waste Act.

Treatment of Hospital Waste

- *General waste.* (Non-toxic, non-infectious): Arrangement must be done with the local Municipality or Corporation for daily removal from a central place.
- *Biomedical waste*: Monitoring of incinerator, autoclave, and microwave must be carried out once in a month, to check the performance of the equipment, and a record be maintained.
- In addition the following will be ensured:
  1. Proper operation and maintenance of the incinerators, autoclaves and microwaves.
  2. While incinerating the, waste proper temperature must be attained in the chambers of the incinerators.
  3. PVC material is not to be incinerated.
  4. Only skilled and trained persons to operate the equipment.
  5. Proper records to be maintained at the incinerator, autoclave, microwave and shredder. Such record will have entries of the period of operation, temperature/pressure obtained, while treating the waste and the quantity of waste treated.
  6. The scavenger will not be allowed to sort out the waste.

7. Proper hygiene will be maintained at the waste treatment site and the storage area.

- *Incineration*: The incinerator must be installed and made operational as per specifications under the Biomedical Waste Act, and an authorization taken from the prescribed authority.
- *Deep Burial*: Standards for deep burial is given in the Biomedical Waste Act. The pit or trench should be about 2 meters deep, should be half filled with waste, and then covered with lime, before filling. On each occasion when waste is added, 190 cm of soil shall be added to cover the waste. There should be no shallow well near the burial site. Deep burial is only permitted in cities, which have less than five lakh population.
- *Autoclave and microwave treatment*: Standards, for autoclaving and microwaving are given in the Act. All equipment installed must meet this specification. The waste under category 3, 4, 6, and 7, can be treated by these methods.
- *Shredding*: The plastics, (IV bottles, IV sets, syringes, catheter), and sharps (Needles, blades, glass etc), should be shredded, only after disinfection by chemical treatment (10 per cent bleaching powder solution) or microwaving or autoclaving.
- Needle destroyers can be used for disposal of needles directly, without chemical treatment.
- *Secured Landfill*: The incinerator ash, discarded medicines, cytoxic substances, and solid chemical waste, should be treated by this method.

- ☆ *Radioactive Waste*: It should be, as per the guidelines issued by the Atomic Research Center.
- ☆ *Liquid and Chemical Waste*: It consists of chemical and liquid waste from the laboratory. Suitable treatment must be given before disposal. The liquid and chemical waste should not be used for any other purpose
- ☆ *Sewerage Waste*: The effluent generated from the hospital, should conform to laid down rules as per the Act.

Collection and Removal

Whatever the final method of disposal, collection is an important factor. The method of collection will depend upon the method of disposal. Collection can be done in waste basket, wheel barrows or in trash carts. Waste baskets made of metal are preferable to others. Flow process of hospital waste is given diagrammatically as under:

INTERIM COLLECTION → TRANSPORTATION → STORAGE → FINAL DISPOSAL

Trash carts should have two sets of containers, wherein after collection of a dirty filled container, an empty clean container is placed in its place. Timing of collection and removal should be convenient to all departments. Collection should be avoided when the patients are resting, or during the normal hospital routine. In a multistoried building, hospital trash is collected at a central point in each floor, and then removed from there for final disposal.

Disposal

Waste disposal is a problem that is assuming alarming proportions. Though there is no evidence that hospital waste has caused disease in the community, it is viewed as hazardous. Whatever be the method of disposal, it has to be carefully chosen and closely monitored. The basic principle is to treat the waste appropriately at the source itself, and then ensuring hygienic conditions, transport to the site of final disposal. The disposal is done as per the color coding.

Thermal Treatment and Incineration

Disposal by burning is the most satisfactory practical method now available in India, though it has its deficiencies. In thermal treatment, the principle is the use of high temperature under pressure. Thermal incineration is preferable, because of its high efficiency in destroying organic material. To make it cost effective, it is normally used on concentrated waste, obtained either by segregation or by physical, chemical and biological methods.

Incinerators are coal fired, oil fired or electrically operated. At present the oil fired incinerators are preferred. A good incinerator must have the capability of converting all materials into nontoxic residue, and is smokeless. It is a must, for disposal of plastic disposables.

Sewage Disposal

In towns and cities, where municipal sewage disposal system is in operation the hospital sewage is directly disposed off into such system. The effluent from the settling tanks of the hospital treatment plant can be safely discharged into the ground. But if it is to be discharged into a stream or river, it has to be chlorinated first.

Safety Measures

Basically it is to preserve the health of those who work

in the area of Bio Medical Waste disposal. Some of the protection measures are given below:

- *Gloves*: The types available are disposable vinyl gloves, latex surgical gloves for invasive procedures and heavy duty rubber gloves up to elbow, for cleaners.
- *Masks*: Simple cloth masks to prevent healthcares workers against aerosols and splashes. Incinerator staff must wear dust masks.
- Protective glasses.
- Plastic aprons.
- Gum boots for hospital waste handlers.
- Immunization against tetanus, and Hepatitis-B.
- Reporting of accidents, and spillages. There should be a procedure for reporting these, and records must be kept.
- All staff must practice universal precautions against HIV virus.
- All sanitation workers engaged in the handling and transporting of hospital waste, should be made aware of the risks involved.

Training

All medical professionals must be made aware of the Biomedical Waste Disposal Rules. Each and every hospital must have well planned awareness program, for all categories of personnel including administrators. Training should be conducted category wise, and in an appropriate language. Training should be interactive, and should have awareness sessions, demonstration sessions, and behavioral science approach sessions. The training is a continuous process and requires periodical refresher training.

Management and Co-ordination

The heads of each hospital must constitute a Waste Management Committee, under his chairmanship. This committee will meet regularly, to review the performance of the waste disposal. It is responsible for making a specific action plan, supervision and monitoring of waste disposal. The head of each hospital is responsible, to take authorization for generation of waste, from appropriate authorities, well in time and to get it renewed, as per the schedule laid down. The committee is also responsible for sending annual reports in time, as well as reporting of accidents.

Co-ordination with Outside Agencies

- *Municipal Authorities*: 90 per cent of the hospital waste comes under the general category and so is to be collected and disposed off by the municipal authorities. So, close co-ordination is required with them.
- Coordinated efforts must be made with the health authorities, and municipal authorities, to involve private sector/NGOs, for creation of common facilities for treatment.
- Coordination with health authorities and NGOs, for public awareness and education.
- Sharing of hospitals having excessive treatment capacity, with smaller hospitals.

- ☆ Coordination with Government Hospital Waste Control agencies. These agencies carry out periodical inspection of Hospital waste disposal arrangements, and their certificate in this regard will require renewal.

Chapter 18

Hospital Infection Control

There is constant danger of patients admitted to the hospital, getting infections while in hospital. It is an irony that patients who come to get their infection cured, end up in getting another infection. Such infections have been divided into Endogenous (opportunistic) and Exogenous. Endogenous infection is derived from the patient's own body, because of the debilitated condition, extremes of age (very young and old), reduced efficacy of the immune system, and breach of skin due to severe burns, skin conditions, surgical intervention etc. This kind of infection can also be the result of infection due to pulmonary infection of patients on respirators, diabetes, secondary to malignancy, and prolonged antibiotic therapy. Exogenous infection is one whose source is external, and is also referred as "cross infection". It is due to improper asepsis, poor sterilization techniques, invasive monitoring and procedures, transmission from hospital staff who are carriers etc.

Hospital infection is the greatest challenge for the patient and the hospital. Because of infection contracted in the hospital, patients are forced to stay in the hospital, longer. The increased lab tests involved and the medication by costly drugs mean tremendous increase in hospital cost. The hospital also suffers from the damage to its reputation, and decreased qualitative utilization of its beds. Hospital infection is also called "nosocomial infection", the English word being derived from the Greek word "Nosokomeion" meaning "Hospital". These are infections that appear in the patient, after 48 hours of admission, infections before 48 hours being considered as contracted from the community. Virulent pathogens are brought in by new patients admitted with infections, in addition to those that exist in the hospital. The two factors which encourage hospital acquired infection are, patients being more susceptible to infection because of their underlying diseases and injuries; and secondly, the increasing trend of bacterial resistance and emergence of new strains.

Extent of the Problem

Various estimates have been given by various authorities, none of them based on controlled studies, regarding the incidence of hospital infection in India. In western countries it is estimated that almost 1/3 of all infections, may be hospital infection. The most reliable estimate for India is that, about 10 per cent of infection in admitted cases could be hospital infection. But one thing is certain; hospital infection occurs in every hospital, only differing in its number. Post-operative wound sepsis occurs in nearly 20 per cent of cases. Although not all such infections can be prevented, data so far gathered indicate, that with a planned effort, it can be reduced to half.

The source of infection is difficult to pin point, as a number of medical and paramedical personnel interact with the patients, who are in various stages of disability. It can be a cross infection from other patients, hospital staff, or visitors. The environments of the hospital also give rise to multiple drug resistant bacteria. In this situation, environmental infection is possible by the patient's contact with toilet fixtures, hospital furniture, crockery, linen, bedpans etc. The third source of infection is, the bacteria carried by the patient himself into the hospital, but which invade his body, because of the decrease in his body resistance, or by procedures done during hospital stay.

The Agent: Almost all the microbes, bacteria, viruses, fungi and protozoa including the opportunistic pathogens which normally reside in our bodies, can be the agent or cause of infection. Almost 25 to 50 per cent of hospital infections are found to be due to gram negative organisms, with almost 10 per cent being due to staphylococci, staphylococcus aureus being predominant. The other organisms involved are pseudomonas (gastro-enteritis, urinary infection, secondary infection in burns), E- coli (catheter related infection), and salmonella, introduced through food carriers. The routes of infection identified are as under:

- ☆ *Droplet infection*: The infection is spread through indiscriminate sneezing, cough, nose blowing.

- ✰ *Contact infection*: By personal contact with another patient, contact with nurses, or via instruments and dressings.
- ✰ *Environmental route*: It may be through contaminated water, food, instruments, or apparatus.
- ✰ *Intravenous route*: Intravenous route is now largely used in modern medicine. The incidence of hospital infection is considerably higher in patients, with peripheral IV devices or central venous catheters.

The highest rate of hospital infection, are in patients subjected to invasive technology. The point to remember is that infected surgical wounds would be sterile on repeated cultures, due to widespread use of antibiotics before surgery. The high risk areas in the hospital are Nurseries, ICUs, Dialysis Center, Burn Unit, Organ Transplant Unit, Isolation Ward, Delivery Rooms and OTs.

Prevention of Hospital Infections

It has been estimated that 50 per cent of these infections are preventable. Some of the important measures are listed below:

1. Conscientious washing of hands by the whole medical team, including doctors and nurses, after contact with the patient. Washing with simple water and soap, will go a long way. Hand washing means vigorous, brief rubbing together, of lathered hands for 10 seconds, followed by rinsing under running water, and not just wetting the hands and casual application of soap.

2. Disinfection of environment, and instruments cum dressings, in all procedures. Sterilization of instruments and consumables are most effective, when done in CSSD. The important ingredients are, use of pre-sterilized packs, disposables, routine periodic disinfection of ward, equipment, furniture, linen etc. But when using disinfectants, we must be clear regarding their effective concentration, and antimicrobial spectrum. The disinfectant used, must be appropriate, must be used in correct concentration, and the contact time must be enough.
3. Adherence to Aseptic techniques. It is very important, when using surgical, and instrumentation procedures. These include use of a "no touch" technique, while changing surgical dressing, periodic insertion/removal of drains, proper maintenance of those who had catheterization etc. Pre-sterilized packs should be used, and sterilized catheters and drains should be periodically removed and inserted.
4. Segregation of Contaminated instruments. They should be kept aside for cleaning, disinfection and repacking, while contaminated material should be incinerated. Soiled linen should be sluiced and washed using steam. Sputum cups, bed pans and urinals to be disinfected as well as autoclaved between uses.
5. Isolation facilities. This must be available in Nurseries, and ICUs, as well as for communicable diseases.

6. Avoiding indiscriminate use of antibiotics. Antibiotics to be used when clearly indicated, in correct dosage and for sufficient period.
7. Staff. They must be immunized against certain diseases, like Typhoid, Hepatitis-B, and screening them for carriers.
8. Surveillance. Continuous scrutiny of patients and procedures must be ensured to determine the type of infections, and why and how they are produced. It requires a system of active follow up of the infections.

Hospital Infection Control Program

The aim is to minimize the risk of hospital infection of a patient, when he is in the hospital. The methods used in the program:

- ☆ Develop an effective surveillance system. This means, that observed data is analyzed and reported to those, who can take action.
- ☆ Develop policies and procedures that reduce the risk of hospital infection.
- ☆ Institute a continuing education program for hospital staff. The program must have certain basic elements:
  - ☆ System for identifying and reporting of infections, as well as keeping records.
  - ☆ System to provide a clean hospital environment, adequate aseptic techniques, and provide effective sterilization and disinfection practices.

- ☆ System to provide effective continuing education to personnel, in infection prevention and control.
- ☆ System for co-ordination with all departments and medical audit committees.

Infection Control Committee (ICC)

The best way to carry out a hospital control program is, to establish such a committee. Its responsibility is to monitor hospital infections, and take appropriate action. The committee must have representatives from main clinical departments, hospital administration, nursing department and the Microbiology department. It must have a Hospital Infection Officer, a specialist in Microbiology, with administrative experience and knowledge of hospital infections, who will act as the secretary. In addition, it must have an Infection Control Nurse, who will be sufficiently senior, and who will carry out the day to day monitoring and surveillance control activities. Preferably the chairman should be the Hospital Administrator. The task of the committee is to lay down policies and procedures in the following:

- ☆ General cleanliness, termite and pest control.
- ☆ Surveillance.
- ☆ Maintenance of proper aseptic techniques.
- ☆ Disinfection procedures.
- ☆ Antibiotic use.
- ☆ Periodical immunization of staff.
- ☆ Conduct of periodic surveillance of statistics.
- ☆ Carry out evaluation of routine surveillance activities.

- ☆ Supervise epidemiological investigations.
- ☆ Review current control practices.
- ☆ Educate staff on infection control program.

Surveillance

The most important aspect of the infection control program is to develop a system of surveillance, to provide systemic and continuous observation of the occurrence of hospital infection. The surveillance system will initially establish a data base, for endemic rates of the infection. The data will include name, age, sex, date of admission, patient hospital No., ward, specialty, date of onset of infection, site of infection, micro-organism isolated, antibiotic sensitivity profile, nature of operating surgery and the surgeon, as well as other invasive procedures (intravascular, urinary, respiratory tract etc.)

Monitoring

It is necessary to monitor the prevalence of cross infection, and initiate corrective measures. Such monitoring is done by:

- ☆ Periodical review of statistics. Statistics of hospital infection is reported in the medical records, and this statistics is compiled by the MRD, or the Infection Control Officer.
- ☆ Ensuring that all cases of infection are reported to the Medical Director.
- ☆ Such intimation allows the hospital administration, to be alerted of any increase in any particular area, identify the source, and to take suitable measures.
- ☆ The Microbiology Department plays a major role in collection and analyzes of lab data on cross

infection. Bacteriological counts and culture and sensitivity tests, of swabs from the patient, the environment, and the appliances in the critical area of the hospital, will provide the nature of the endemic prevalence of microorganisms responsible, and the antibiotics to be used.

- ☆ Depending on the nature of the organism, the source of infection, mode of transmission, and the severity of the infection the following actions can be taken:
  1. Modify the nature of carrying out certain procedures, like type of sterile pack used, preference for use of disposable material as compared to reusable, use of antiseptic techniques, use of different chemical disinfectant, better disposal of infected material etc.
  2. Isolate the patient to limit the spread of the particular infection.
  3. Disinfect the environment by fumigation or aerosol.
  4. Adopt Universal precautionary measures.

Effective Control Measures

People

It is the people in hospitals, rather than the physical environment which constitute the infection reservoir. Conscientious hand washing between contacts with patients is the most effective remedy in this regard. All areas in the hospital must have, hand washing facilities.

Adoption of Universal Precautions

This must be practiced in all areas. The components of universal precautions are:

1. Hand washing. This is most important for newborns and young infants.
2. Careful handling of sharp objects.
3. Sterilization or disinfection of instruments
4. Using protective items like gowns, aprons, gloves, masks, and protective eye wear (goggles).
5. Restricted entry to special areas like ICUs, OTs, Burn Units, nurseries.
6. Double gloving and use of boots in OT.
7. Isolation of patients with communicable diseases.
8. Isolation of cases in Pandemic or Epidemic situations.

Aseptic Techniques

Aseptic techniques must be strictly insisted upon in various invasive procedures. Insertion and removal of catheters, surgical tubing, drainage tubes, and surgical packing, must use "no touch" technique, even when done in the OPD.

Segregation of Contaminated Instruments

The segregation of contaminated (used) Instruments from others must be strictly insisted upon. A system must be put in place for keeping the contaminated pieces of linen, sputum cups, bed pans, urinals, and similar items separately, so that it does not get mixed up with the clean items.

Disinfection Practices

Different kinds of disinfectants vary in their reaction to different microorganisms. Selection of appropriate disinfectants, using them in the correct concentration, and ensuring optimum period of exposure, will give results. Chemical disinfectants are best avoided, when heat infection is possible.

Sterilization Practices

Sterilization and infection can be by four methods namely sterilization by steam, sterilization by dry heat, boiling for ten minutes, and disinfection by chemicals. But an efficient CSSD is the practical answer. If sterilization in flash sterilizers in OT becomes unavoidable, it must be done by trained personnel.

Isolation Facilities

Such facilities have to be provided for those suffering from communicable diseases, or for those vulnerable to infection, like those in Nurseries, ICUs, Burn Units and Organ Transplant Units. Strict control of wearing of gowns, masks, and gloves, and change of slippers (foot wear) must be ensured.

Antibiotic Policy

The major problem is the involvement of organisms, with multiple resistances. Culture and sensitivity tests must be a routine. The factors that influence anti biotic resistance are, volume of antibiotic use, extensive use of certain antibiotics when not essential, and use of antibiotics in a prophylactic role.

Out Patient Department

Must have separate arrangements for examining patients with communicable diseases.

Dietary Services

Refrigerators and deep freezers must be checked for its efficiency. Efficient pest rodent control must be assured.

Soiled Linen

All soiled linen must be treated as potentially infective. Such linen must be packed in separate bags, before taking to the laundry, and there, it must be processed separately.

Good Housekeeping

Cleaning of walls, floors, window panes, window sills, bedside screens and tables, curtains, and bathroom fixtures, and use of appropriate disinfectants after cleaning, must be done in a systematic manner.

Terminal Disinfection

Terminal disinfection of rooms used by highly infective patients must be thorough, as done in OT, before another patient is admitted.

Air Hygiene in Operation Theaters

Periodic checking and cleaning of air filters must be done, and smoke studies should be carried out, for air movement.

Training

Training and retraining has to be done for the staff in precautionary measures, prevention and control.

Prevention of Spread of HIV and AIDS

Statistics show that there is an increasing trend of such infections, specially in third world countries. Hence prevention of the spread of these infections, have assumed paramount importance:

- ☆ Test specimens, must be dispatched only in sealed watertight containers.
- ☆ Double gloving is the mandatory requirement, when dealing with such patients.
- ☆ Gowns must be worn specially when there is risk of contact with secretions, or blood.
- ☆ Face masks are not normally necessary for patients. But for patients with cough, use of masks is recommended.
- ☆ Use of goggles, especially by dentists when treating such patients.
- ☆ Washing of hands after contact with such patients. Surfaces and furniture, contaminated by blood or body fluids, should be treated with a disinfectant.
- ☆ Use of disposable syringes and needles are recommended. Used consumables, and linen should be soaked in bleaching solution, as per the rules for biomedical waste, before disposal.
- ☆ Disposables for mouth to mouth resuscitation must be available at the bedside.
- ☆ All instruments, including thermometers, must be soaked in bleaching water solution, and then sterilized before reuse.
- ☆ Accommodation. Not necessary to isolate such patients in single isolation rooms.

- ☆ *Surgery*. As a general rule all cases taken up for surgery should be treated as potential HIV or AIDS infected, and universal protection measures should be adopted.

Chapter 19
Medical Ethics

Medical ethics is derived from values in health care. It is concerned with the obligations of the doctor and the hospital, towards the patient, other health professionals and the society. Ethics is not static, and what was considered good ethics ten years back, may not be so today. A hospital administrator has to face many ethical problems in his daily functioning. The medical ethics often involve matters of life and death, patients rights, informed consent, confidentiality, competence, negligence and so on. Medical ethics is in a flux today in India. There is a school of thought, who holds that these days, when morality and ethical considerations, are forgotten thoughts, why harp on professional ethics. It is exactly because of these falling standards, that we have to emphasize professional ethics.

The Hippocrates oath which all doctors take on registration has now been simplified by the Declaration of

Geneva, and many countries have adopted their own codes, bases on this declaration. The Indian Code of Ethics is also based on this declaration. The general content of this code of conduct are:

1. Maintain high standards of professional conduct.
2. Medical practice must not be wholly based on motives of profit.
3. Unethical practices, like self advertisement, collaboration with service where the doctor does not have professional independence and prohibition of receiving monetary or other considerations, other than professional fees.

The problems are:

1. Those concerning professional activities of the doctors.
2. Those concerning informed consent and right of patients.
3. Those involving social justice and equity, including use of sophisticated technology, and experiments on human beings.
4. Those pertaining to the right to life.
5. Commercialization of health services.

The values in health care have an hierarchy of its own. The conventional hierarchy is:

- ✰ Preservation of life.
- ✰ Relief of pain and suffering.
- ✰ Cure of disease.
- ✰ Care of person.

- ✰ Prevention of disease.
- ✰ Promotion of health

This prioritization has been questioned, mainly on the ground that promotion of health must get a higher priority. In earlier days, the people had unbounded trust in doctors. This situation is changing, and the patients and the community are questioning the action of the doctors. Patients have started asserting their rights. Many countries and consumer organizations have started to insist on a bill of rights for the patients. The inclusion of medical practice under the Consumer Protection Act, has further augmented, the cry for a bill of patient's right, in developing countries like India, based on the American Bill of Rights. This is under the active consideration of the Indian Central Government.

We will now have a look at the usual problem areas, in which ethical consideration play a part.

Informed Consent

Consent is implied when a patient presents himself to a doctor for examination and treatment. Its absence, if alleged, will have to be proved by the patient. But there used to be a belief, that to get an informed consent from patients hailing from a rural areas of under developed countries, is difficult, because of rampant illiteracy. This has been proved to be false, and all that is required is, that he must be told the facts in simple terms, in a language he understands, and with patience. The question usually rises whether a doctor can withhold treatment, if there is no informed consent? The conflict is between the moral duty of the doctor and the legal right of the patient. Can a man refrain from benefiting from medical treatment and forfeit his life? On the contrary, what about the patients right to determine, what shall be done to him? What is the status of "informed consent", when a patient is admitted in a critical stage?

The reasonable solution when a patient does not give informed consent is to seek the help of relatives and friends. As far as a critical patient is concerned, there is a ruling from the High Court of the Kerala state of India, that when a patient life is in danger, the doctor must proceed without consent, getting another doctor to certify the criticality, and witnessed by the hospital administrator. This seems to be the consensus in most countries.

Medical Treatment and Procedures

The legal privileges and limitations of the medical staff must be known by all members of the health team. Accepted Diagnostic and therapeutic procedures, which are commonly accepted, and practiced in good faith is upheld by law. However hospitals must be careful to select staff who are qualified and competent, and who are legally registered.

Refusal of Treatment by Doctors and Hospitals

Every doctor and hospital has the paramount obligation to prevent loss of life or prolong it. No law can contravene this paramount duty. All hospitals must provide aid to all cases, irrespective of the fact that it is a medico-legal case, and treatment cannot and should not wait for legal documentary formalities. Medical Councils of various countries have also pointed out, that there is no law which compels a doctor to delay rendering care to a serious patient, so as to wait for the arrival of the police. The hospital and the doctor is legally bound to treat a patient, and if they do not do so, they are liable to punishment.

Confidentiality

Considerable confidential information, will come to the notice of the medical care team, and must be treated as fully confidential. It can be shared with the other members of the team, only to the extent necessary, or as required by law. Moreover patients medical records are the property of the patient, and the hospital is only the custodian. Some times access to the medical records is asked for by the patient. In such cases, discretion is used in allowing access, to the relevant portion of the records which contribute to better understanding, after consultation with the treating doctor. A Bombay High Court (India) ruling gives the patient, the right to a copy of his medical records.

Defective Equipment

It is the responsibility of the hospital to ensure that its equipment is in working condition. If injury or death occurs, because of defective equipment, the hospital will be liable. This is also applicable to the bed rails and side rails of hospital beds, meant for avoidance of injury to patients. If these are not properly fixed, and if the patient suffers an injury because of this deficiency, the hospital becomes liable. Apart from the legal aspect, the ethical considerations will also come into play.

Unethical Advertisement

Earlier, advertising in hospitals was frowned upon. But now marketing with advertisement is a normal aspect of hospital functioning. The ruie of thumb is, advertising a department of a hospital is ethical, but highlighting an individual doctor, is unethical. Advertising regarding a doctor newly joining the hospital, or rejoining after absence, is ethical. All are agreed that certain advertisements are not ethical:

- ☆ If it contains misrepresentation of facts.
- ☆ If it claims that own professional skills are better than that of other hospitals.
- ☆ Contains exaggerated claims.
- ☆ Media Supplements issued by hospitals, which in addition to departments, also gives the name of individual doctors.

Some of the acceptable advertisements are:

- ☆ Informing about the type of services offered by the hospital.
- ☆ Informing about addition to departments or specialties.
- ☆ Informing about the different specialties available, without naming the consultants.
- ☆ Informing about insurance facilities available.
- ☆ Rejoining of consultants, after absence.
- ☆ New consultants initially joining the hospital.

Diagnostic Aids

There is a growing market for sophisticated diagnostic equipment. Many times, developing countries are used as dumping grounds for obsolete equipment, no more usable in developed countries. Moreover when such equipment is purchased from abroad by developing countries, there is difficulty in their servicing and maintenance. Doctors trained in developed countries, on return to their developing countries put pressure on the hospital administration to buy sophisticated equipment, even though realities point otherwise. Again when these equipment go out of order, there is no back up service, and they lie idle. Is it ethical for doctors and hospitals of India to buy such equipment, not fully necessary, using up precious foreign exchange? Is it ethical for a firm to sell these equipments, without ensuring proper back up? These are ethical questions which require to be debated.

Drugs and Pharmaceuticals

There is a huge proliferation of drugs in the market, mostly in third world countries like India. Many of these drugs are manufactured by tiny factories, on a "loan license" basis. These small factories are not subject to the stringent standards applicable to the large ones. These products are then marketed by the larger companies, under their brand name.

There are many drugs banned in foreign countries which are sold in the Indian market. There are drugs banned in Indian market, which are still sold, because of the "stay orders" by the courts. Legal proceedings take considerable time, and during this period, doctors continue to prescribe these hazardous drugs. Again many of the drugs in the market are substandard, a survey showing that 20 to 25 per cent of the drugs are substandard. Another alarming aspect is the tendency of doctors, to over prescribe, or to prescribe "glamorous" drugs. The drug companies also push the doctors in prescribing their drugs, by any means. If the doctors become ethical in prescribing, there would be no market for irrational drug therapy.

Manufacturers are by law, required to give the indications, contraindications, and the side effects of their drugs. They do so, but in many cases, in a way that will not attract attention. As a wag said "the greater the danger, the smaller the print". The pricing of drugs is also another area of concern. The Maximum Retail Price (MRP) is laid down by the manufacturers. There is large variation in MRP of drugs used for critical care in developing countries. The respective governments require to go into this.

Gift giving, by the medical companies, is rampant in many countries. This raises many ethical questions.

Health Policy

The questions that rise in this regard are:

- Who shall receive what health care?
- What is the standard in setting priorities?
- What is a "standard" of good health care?
- How do we decide on allocation of resources?
- Who should decide the health policy?
- Is equal utilization of health care services according to the need, the best way of ensuring equity?

Drug Trials

This is essential for any research, and without research, there can be no progress. But in hospitals where investigational drugs are used, it should be done under the supervision of a "Research Committee". The informed consent of patients participating in the trials must be taken, the emphasis being on "Informed Consent". In the case of double blind studies, where the patient and the staff are not aware which drug is being given at any particular time, the code of the double blind study, should be immediately available to the treating physician, to enable him to counteract any untoward reactions.

Invasion of Privacy

Disregard of patient's right to personal privacy in patients who are unable to protect themselves, because of unconsciousness, disability or immobility, is legally actionable. But there are many instances of invasion of privacy in hospitals. Some times because the patient is old, there is no care for his personal privacy, and certain procedures are done without due care for personal privacy. Unjustified intrusion into the private domain of the patient, and taking pictures of the patient without their permission, are against medial ethics.

Operation Theater Procedures

Some times partly covered female patients are handled in Operation Theaters, by male medical aids. This is against medical ethics.

Right to Life

It is accepted that every human being has the right to life. But the ethical questions are many. When do we call an entity a human being? Does a "person" start from the formation of the zygote, produced from the time of the union of the sperm and ovum, and is individuality reckoned from that time? What is the role of "soul" in this regard?

Abortion

Many third world countries allows abortion, if the continuation of pregnancy poses a grave risk to the mother's life, or her physical and mental health. But the question is, abortion may be legal, but is it "moral". Is abortion, as an instrument of population control, ethical? In abortion there is a conflict of the right of two persons, whom the mother and the growing fetus. Has the mother the right to destroy the life of the child, she is carrying in her womb? Is the child a "possession", which the mother can "dispose off", without consideration for the right of the unborn child. In the context of rising demand for fetal tissues in the treatment of Parkinsonism, is it ethical for the doctor, to participate in abortions, which may have an element of financial consideration.

Infanticide

If a newborn is detected with deformities incompatible with life, should we terminate pregnancy or await for the fetus to be born? If the defects are compatible with life, what then? In countries like India, it is our experience, that many families accept such children, as a part of their life or karma (fate), but in other cases, is abortion ethical?

Euthanasia

Hasn't a person the right to quit life, which according to him, is not worth living? Is the right to die implicit in the right to live? Legally euthanasia is not permitted in many countries. But to stop life supporting systems, or not to adopt heroic measures to prolong life, in terminally ill patients, are considered ethical.

Disclosure of Information

Doctors differ in their approach, as to how much and when to tell the truth, to a dying patient. The conflicting considerations are the right of the patient to know, and the possible benefit if the patient knows the truth, versus the harm we may do by disclosing the truth. The practical approach is to involve the relatives in the process, and if in doubt, tell the truth.

In conclusion it would be appropriate to enumerate the code of conduct expected from the doctor:

- ☆ Must conduct himself with dignity and propriety.
- ☆ Must update his knowledge continuously.
- ☆ Should not solicit patients either directly or indirectly.
- ☆ Should not exhibit any advertising material in his consulting room.
- ☆ Formal advertisement should be restricted to start of practice, or change of address.
- ☆ Do not enter into any agreement for "no cure, no payment".
- ☆ Should not give or receive any commission for referring cases.
- ☆ Should not prescribe any secret medicine, or Ayurvedic medicine or Homeopathic medicine.
- ☆ Should not lend his name for advertisement or publicity.
- ☆ There is no rule that physicians should not charge professional fees from another physician. It is only a professional courtesy.

Chapter 20
Material Management

No book on hospital supporting systems can be completed without a look at material management. Material management is concerned with two main sections namely the Purchase section and the Stores section. These sections must be separated, each one headed by a separate officer of suitable rank. Both these come under the medical superintend or the medical director. The purchase section is directly supervised by the Purchase Officer. This section is responsible for compilation of demands, finalization of specifications, floating of tenders, placement of supply order, monitoring of liabilities,, record keeping regarding payment of bills, etc.

The store section is supervised by a Store Officer, who is good in material management. The store keepers and other staff work under him. He is responsible for initiation of demands, receipt of goods, testing and quality control, record keeping in stock ledgers, bill verification, issue of goods, ensuring continuous and uninterrupted supply (avoiding stock out position). This section should formulate its own Standing Operating Procedures. The inventory of the hospital should preferably be maintained on computer.

The officers of the purchase and store department, should be turned over every two years to prevent them acquiring any vested interest, and should have training in material management.

Equipment Maintenance and Repair

A separate section should be established in each hospital, to deal with maintenance and repair of equipment, headed by a bio medical engineer, if such a post exists. A committee should be instituted, to finalize the contracts for maintenance and repair. The tenders should preferably be on the "double bid system". All sophisticated systems should be under the annual maintenance system. A history sheet should be maintained for each expensive item indicating cost, date of purchase, source of purchase, details and cost of repairs done, period when equipment remained out of order etc. A periodic review of status of functioning of all equipment, should be done at the highest level, and the status of all important equipment, should be displayed.

Annual Physical Stock Verification

The responsibility for this is of the head of the department, and is done by deputing various officers. The ground balance should be checked with the ledger balance, and initialed. Major losses or surplus must be reported to the head of the institution.

Material Condemnation

A condemnation board should be constituted periodically, at least every three months, to condemn the non-consumable items. This board should declare, items condemned after proper scrutiny, giving directions regarding their disposal. After completion of action, proper ledger entries should be made.

Material Management Analyses

Only two methods will be discussed.

ABC Analyses

Rather than trying to manage simultaneously all items, an impossible task, it helps in giving priority to selected items to give maximum results. Identification of these items is based not only on the unit cost, or the relative quantity consumed, but on its annual consumption value, which is a combination of both. From experience we know that 5-10 per cent of all items (called A category), account for 70 per cent of annual consumption costs, another 10 to 20 per cent (called B category) account for 20 per cent of the costs, and the balance 70 per cent account for the remaining 5 to 10 per cent of cost. By concentrating on the A category, 70 per cent results can be achieved.

However in pharmacy it has been found that VED analyses are more effective. Items are classified as vital, essential and desirable based upon their stock out costs. V items require a large safety stock(reserve), while D items can do with little reserve.

Issue/Distribution

The two methods used are periodical issue through indents, say once a week, or as and when necessary as replacement. The latter is preferable for expensive drugs and expensive consumables.

Usage

Savings by inventory control is small as compared to savings that accrue by economic use of materials. Particular care should be taken to ensure that there is no over preparation of items which have a limited shelf life.

Chapter 21

Laws Applicable to Hospitals–I

The laws applicable to hospitals, can be broadly divided into two; one, laws applicable to Institutions and Organizations in general, and applicable to hospitals also; and two, laws applicable to hospitals only. In this chapter we are only dealing with the laws applicable to Institutions and Organizations in general, and applicable to the hospitals also, and will be dealing with laws exclusively applicable to hospitals, in the subsequent chapter. The general laws applicable to hospitals are:

- ☆ Industrial Disputes Act.
- ☆ Payment of Wages Act.
- ☆ Minimum Wages Act.
- ☆ Maternity Benefit act.

- Employment Exchange (compulsory notification of vacancies) Act.
- Payment of Bonus Act.
- Payment of Gratuity Act.
- Employees Provident Fund Act.
- Contract Labor Act
- Trade Union Act.
- Workmen's Compensation Act.
- Festival and National Holidays Act.

Industrial Disputes Act

The hospital has been categorized as an "Industry "and so this act is applicable to the hospitals. The object of the act is to amicably settle the conflicts between the employer and employee, and to make provisions for problems, that may rise in day to day functioning of industries. The act does not discourage collective bargaining, but provides the machinery, to ensure that normal functioning is not disrupted. It provides for payment of compensation to workman, in the event of retrenchment, layoff or closure.

Definitions

Any act is based on certain definitions, and some of them are enumerated below. It must be read in conjunction with the Act.

- *Closure*: Permanent closing down of a place of employment, or part thereof. It is a "permanent" closing down. It is not necessary that the whole establishment has been closed down. The closure can be partial also.

- *Conciliation Officer*: One who is appointed under the provisions of the Act, and who is required to promote settlement of disputes.
- *Profit Motive*: Its absence is not relevant as far as this act is concerned.
- *Industrial Dispute*: Dispute between an employer and employee, between a employee and another, connected with employment or non-employment, or connected with conditions of labor.
- *Lock out*: Temporary closing down of a place of work, or the refusal of the employer, to employ a specified number of employees.
- *Lay off*: Means failure, refusal or inability of the employer, because of shortage of certain essential items like power, and raw material, or due to breakdown of machinery or due to natural calamities, to give employment to a workman, born on the muster rolls.
- *Retrenchment*: Termination of services, but excludes termination as a punishment, or voluntary retirement or retiring on reaching the age of superannuation, or on grounds of ill health, or due to non-renewal of contract.
- *Settlement*: Settlement arrived at during the process of conciliation, or a written agreement between the employer and workman, signed by both.
- *Strike*: Cessation of work, by a body of employees. It is not necessary that the stoppage of work is total, and partial stoppage would also be strike. But if an individual absents himself, for enforcing his

demand for higher pay, it is not strike, as the clause "body of employees", is not satisfied.

- *Workman*: Any person including an "apprentice", employed in an industry, to do any kind of work. In this case, the term of employment, can be express or implied. The term does not include, those employed mainly in a managerial, or administrative capacity.
- *Public Utility*: Includes railway, ports, P&T services, power supply installations, or sanitary services.

Investigation and Settlement Authorities

The act provides for certain statutory authorities, who have the authority to investigate and settle disputes:

1. *Works Committee*: It is applicable to industries, or hospitals employing 100 workers or more. The committee includes elected worker representatives, and an equal number of representatives of employer.
2. *Board of Conciliation*: Consists of an independent chairman, and two or four members from the employees, and equal number from the management.
3. *Labor Courts or Industrial Tribunals*: Constituted by the government, for adjucation, if the efforts of the Conciliation Officer, has failed. Reference to a labor court is, when not more than 100 workmen are affected. If 100 or more workers are affected, the reference is to a industrial tribunal.
4. *Voluntary Arbitration*: There is provision for the two parties to seek voluntary arbitration, if there is

mutual agreement. But such agreement for voluntary arbitration, must be made before the case is referred to the labor court, or the tribunal.

Strikes and Lockouts

Strikes and lockouts are covered by section 22 and 23 of the act. The provisions are:

Strike

No person employed in a utility service, can go on a strike with out fulfilling the following conditions.

- ☆ Without giving the employer a notice within six weeks before striking.
- ☆ Within 14 days of giving such notice.
- ☆ Before the expiry of the date given in any other notice.
- ☆ During the pendancy of conciliatory proceedings, and seven days of conclusion of such proceedings.

Lockout

No employer carrying out any public utility service, shall lockout any of his workmen:

- ☆ Without giving them notice, within six weeks of lockout or
- ☆ Within 14 days of giving such notice or
- ☆ Before the expiry of the date of lockout specified in any notice given or
- ☆ During the pendency of any conciliation proceedings.

General Prohibition of Strikes and Lockouts

No workman shall go on strike or any employer declare a lockout:

- ☆ During the pendancy of any conciliation proceedings, and within seven days after the conclusion of such proceedings.
- ☆ During the pendancy of proceedings before a court, tribunal or national tribunal, and within two months after conclusion of such proceedings.
- ☆ During the pendancy of arbitration and within two months after the conclusion of the arbitration proceedings.
- ☆ During the period in which a settlement or award, is in operation.

Penalty for Illegal Strikes or Lockouts

Any workman who commences or continues an illegal strike or promotes such a strike, is punishable by, imprisonment up to one month, or fine up to 50 rupees, or both. Any employer who commences or continues an illegal lockout, or promotes any such lockout, shall be punishable by, imprisonment up to one month, or fine up to 1000 rupees, or both. Any person, who instigates or incites an illegal strike or lockout, is punishable with imprisonment up to one month or fine up to 1000 rupees or both. Government can prohibit the commencement or continuance of a strike, for investigation and adjudication of the dispute, subject to the conditions stated in the act.

Lay Off

An employer has the right to lay off, subject to the conditions given in the definition, of lay off. But the workman is entitled to compensation for the period. The conditions for lay off are as under:

- Must be a justified layoff.
- Employer must maintain a muster roll of the workman.
- Stoppage of work during working hours must be put up on notice board.
- The period of lay off, during working hours, should not exceed two hours after commencement of the stoppage.
- If the lay off is for a short period, to be regularized as compulsory leave.
- If lay off is for indefinite period, services may be terminated, by giving pay in lieu of notice.
- The employees must be informed, whether he is to remain in his pace of work or leave it, when work will be resumed, and the time when workers have to present themselves, for work during normal working hours.
- When not able to specify the period of lay off, the worker must be given three weeks to rejoin duty, when work is resumed. When the workers are called back to work, the union should be informed.
- Quantum of compensation.
    1. If lay off occurs during working hours, and if the period of detention, does not exceed one hour, no payment for period of detention.
    2. If period of detention exceeds one hour, payment for the whole time of detention.

3. Workman who have completed not less than one year of continuous service, when laid off, have to be paid for the full period of lay off, except for such weekly holidays that may intervene. The rate is 50 per cent of the total of basic wages, and dearness allowance. But if the period of lay off exceeds 45 days during any period of twelve months, no compensation is required to be paid after 45 days, if there is an agreement between the employer and workman, to that effect. It will be lawful for the employer to retrench the worker, paying his stipulated dues, after the 45 days.

Retrenchment

Retrenchment means discharge of surplus labor or staff. It is not necessary that the discharge of surplus staff, should be only if there is a loss. But the retrenchment must be just and fair. Re-organization of business, economy, etc is good reasons for retrenchment. The retrenchment must fulfill certain conditions, as given in section 25F of the Act:

- ☆ Retrenchment must be by termination of employment.
- ☆ One month notice or pay in lieu of should be given, specifying the date of retrenchment.
- ☆ Employee must be paid compensation of 15 days pay for each year of completed service.
- ☆ Employer must fulfill following conditions in this regard.
  1. Must maintain a muster roll.
  2. Must prepare a seniority list in the category from which retrenchment is being done.

3. The junior most employee must be retrenched first.
4. The retrenched staff has the right to get the first employment, which may rise after retrenchment.

Transfer of Undertaking

When a hospital ownership is transferred to another owner, every employee, who has been in continuous service for not less than one year, is entitled to notice and payment as if he has been retrenched. However this provision will not be applicable if:

- ☆ Services of the workman, have not been interrupted by such a transfer.
- ☆ Terms of service are not less favorable after the transfer.
- ☆ The new employer undertakes to pay compensation, if the employee is retrenched, as if his service has been a continuous one, and not interrupted by the transfer.

Closure

It has been defined in the act. In essence it means, closing down a place of employment either wholly or partially. Closure is a fundamental right of the employer, and nobody can be forced to carry on his business, against his will. But closure must be permanent, though the employer, can re-start his business later. Closure of a department of a hospital is valid, as long as the intention is to close it down, permanently. However the employer must pay the laid down compensation. The following conditions apply:

- ☆ Every workman, who has been in continuous service, for not less than one year, at the date of closure, has to be paid, as if he was retrenched.
- ☆ If the undertaking is closed down for reasons beyond the control of the employer, the compensation paid is not more than average pay of three months. Financial difficulties, accumulation of undisposed stock, expiry of lease or license, are not reasons for closure, under the term "unavoidable circumstance".
- ☆ If the hospital has 50 workers or more, sixty days notice has to be given by the employer, to the government, clearly stating the reasons for the closure.

Controls

If the hospital has 300 or more workman, prior approval of the government is necessary before retrenchment, closure or layoff. If the hospital is employing 100 workman or more, governments prior permission is required for layoff, under special provisions. However, if refusal of permission has not been intimated within two months, it will be assumed that permission has been given.

Miscellaneous Matters

1. During the pendancy of any conciliation proceedings, no action will be taken to alter the conditions of service, award punishment in matters relating to the dispute, or similar action.
2. Protected workman. Any workman, who is an officer of a registered union, and recognized as such, under the rules. The total number of

protected workman cannot exceed, one per cent of the total workmen.

Payment of Wages Act

The act guarantees payment of wages in time, and without deductions, other than authorized ones. The act makes the employer responsible for payment of wages, fixation of wage period, time and mode of payment of wages, and permissible deductions. Under this act:

- ☆ *Wages*: Remuneration including overtime, holiday and leave period.
- ☆ *Timely Payment*: Wages must be paid before the expiry of the seventh day, of the wage period, on a working day. In case of termination wages must be paid on the second day of such a termination. No wage period should exceed one month.
- ☆ *Deduction from Wages*: The accepted deductions are fines, period of absence, deduction for damages directly attributed to the employee, for house accommodation, deduction for interest on advances or loans, for income tax, premium of life insurance policies, or those due to written authorization. Fines should not exceed 3 per cent of the wages in a month.

Minimum Wages Act

The act has been passed to fix minimum wages, so as to avoid exploitation of labor. The wages are fixed for different category of employees, and the act is implemented by both the central government and the state government. It consists of the following:

1. A basic rate of wages.
2. Dearness allowance or cost of living allowance. It is revised periodically.
3. Cash value of concessions.
4. Hours of work. Not to exceed 9 hours per day. Any work over and above 9 hours a day or more than 48 hours in a week, will entitle the employee for overtime. Overtime is, double the normal rates.
5. Rest day. One day of rest in a week.

Employers are required to keep the following records:

- ☆ Register of wages containing minimum wages payable, number of days employee worked including overtime, gross wages, deductions, wages actually paid with signature of employee etc.
- ☆ Register of overpayment in Form IV.
- ☆ Muster Roll in Form V.
- ☆ Register of fines in Form I
- ☆ Register for deductions for damages.
- ☆ Put up a notice in Form XIII, showing the minimum wages payable.
- ☆ Exhibit an extract of the act on the notice board.
- ☆ Give annual return in Form XII to the labor commissioner.

This act is applicable to all hospitals and is irrespective of the fact whether the hospital is in a financial position to pay the wages stipulated in the act.

Maternity Benefit Act

This is to protect the health of a working woman mother, during pregnancy. It is applicable to hospital employing 10 or more employees. The following definitions are important:

- Child includes a still born child.
- Delivery-birth of a child.
- Wages–all remuneration including dearness allowance, house rent, incentive bonus, and money value of any concessional supply. Does not include, any bonus other than incentive bonus, overtime, or payment to pension fund or provident fund.

Prohibition of Work

No woman will knowingly be employed within the six weeks following her delivery, or miscarriage.

Entitlement

- The employee must have worked in the hospital, for a period of not less than 80 days, in the twelve months, immediately preceding her expected date of delivery.
- She will be entitled to a total of twelve weeks, at the rate of average daily wages. The average daily wages is calculated by dividing the monthly wages by 25. The period of leave will be not more than 6 weeks before delivery, and the rest after delivery. The point is that maternity leave cannot be more than six weeks before date of delivery, but the leave after delivery can be more than six weeks, the total not to exceed 12 weeks. If no prenatal or post natal

care is provided by the hospital, the woman is entitled to a bonus of Rs 250.

- A woman suffering from illness arising out of pregnancy, delivery or miscarriage, will be entitled, on production of proof, to an additional one months leave with pay.
- Every woman returning to duty after delivery, is entitled to two nursing breaks, of 15 minutes each, to feed her child during her working hours. This is until the child reaches the age of 15 months.
- In the event of miscarriage, the woman is entitled to six weeks maternity leave, following the date of her miscarriage.
- In cases of tubectomy, a woman is entitled to two weeks leave, with pay.
- The dismissal or discharge of a woman during her pregnancy, is not permissible, under normal circumstances.

Procedure for Applying for Maternity Leave

Any woman worker entitled to maternity leave must apply in writing for maternity benefits. She may nominate a close relative to accept payment. In the application, she must give an undertaking that she will not work in any establishment during her maternity leave. She must also produce a medical certificate, indicating her probable date of delivery. On receipt of this application, indicating the date she wants pre delivery leave, she will be granted the same and she will be paid her wages for the pre-delivery leave, provided it does not exceed six weeks. Immediately on delivery, she should inform her employer of the date of delivery. On receipt of this, she should be granted her post delivery leave, and dues within 48 hours. The total pre delivery leave and post delivery leave cannot exceed 12 weeks.

This Act has attracted attention in the context of certain organizations delaying appointment of selected women candidates on the ground that they are pregnant.

Employment Exchange (Compulsory Notification of Vacancies) Act

Compulsory notification of all vacancies to the employment exchange, is now required under the law. But selection of workman rests with the employer, and he is free to call upon other sources also. This is applicable to private sector also. However this act is not applicable to any employment less than three months or for unskilled office work. However, the fact that the vacancy has been notified, do not impose an obligation on the employer, to recruit or fill vacancies, from the list provided by the employment exchange.

The vacancies are to be notified in writing, at least one week before the vacancy is to be filled, or the applicants are to be interviewed, giving the following particulars:

- ☆ Name, telephone number and address of the employer.
- ☆ Name of vacancy-type of work required (designation), description of duties, qualification required (essential and desirable), age limit, whether women are eligible, number of vacancies (regular, temporary), pay and allowances, place of work, probable date when vacancy will be filled,

details regarding date of interview (date of interview, time and place, designation of the person to whom the applicant must report), any category who will be given preference etc.

Returns are also required to be furnished to the local employment exchange, quarterly returns in Form ER-I and biannual returns in Form ER-II.

It has been repeatedly reported that the hospitals are not following the provisions of this act.

Payment of Bonus Act

Applicable to hospitals, employing not less than 20 persons. Persons mean any other than apprentice, but only include those who are in receipt of pay less than Rs 3500 per month. This upper ceiling of salary is bound to be revised from time to time. The employee must have worked for not less than 30 days in the accounting year. The minimum bonus, even if the hospital is making a loss, is 8.33 per cent, the maximum is 20 per cent of the salary or wages. The salaries of those in the salary range of Rs 2500 to Rs 3500 per month, will be deemed to be Rs 2500 for the purpose of this act. In the first five years of establishment of the hospital, this act will only be applicable to the accounting year, in which there is a profit. It is not applicable to hospitals, which are established "not for profit".

Dearness allowance is included in the definition of salary, but overtime is not included. An employee, who is dismissed from service on grounds of fraud, riotous or violent behavior, or theft, or misappropriation, or sabotage, is disqualified from receiving the bonus, not only for the accounting year, but for any balance of bonus due to him, in the previous years.

Payment of Gratuity Act

It is applicable to hospitals, in which 10 or more persons are employed, during the previous 12 months. At present, the salary limit for gratuity has been removed, but the total amount of gratuity has been restricted to Rs 100000. Gratuity is payable on termination of service, after he has completed 5 years of continuous service, which is usually:

1. On his superannuation.
2. On his retirement or resignation.
3. On his death or disablement. On death, gratuity will have to be paid even if the employee has not completed 5 years of service.

Rate of Gratuity

15 days wages, based on the rate of wages last drawn by the employee. The following requires to be noted:

1. For arriving at daily wages, the monthly salary is divided by 25.
2. In case of piece-rated employee, daily wages to be computed on an average of the total wages received by him, for period of three months immediately preceding termination.
3. In case of seasonal employees, who are employed in a seasonal establishment, and not through out the year, the rate of gratuity is seven days wages for each season.
4. Wages means all emoluments, including dearness allowance, but excludes bonus, commission, house rent allowance, overtime, or any other allowances.

5. Gratuity paid during the lifetime of the employee cannot be attached. But if it is paid on the death of an employee it is attachable.
6. The gratuity has to be paid within 30 days of it becoming payable. It has to be paid by cash or by demand draft.
7. If no gratuity is paid, it should be claimed within one year of it becoming due.
8. Gratuity can be forfeited, if the service is terminated for riotous conduct, or disorderly conduct, or any act of violence, or on charges of moral turpitude.
9. There is a statutory obligation, to display notice in a conspicuous place, at the entry of the hospital, in a language understood by the employees, giving the designation of officer to whom, the application for gratuity is to be given.
10. The maximum gratuity payable is Rs. 2.5 lakhs.

Employees Provident Fund Act (PF Act)

It applies, to hospitals, employing 20 or more persons. The act is applicable to only those employees who are in receipt of pay, including dearness allowance, which is not in excess of Rs 5000 per month. Earlier, this act was not applicable to hospitals, until they complete 3 years of their existence, but it is now applicable from day one. The provident fund act is also applicable to the employees of any contractor, employed by the hospital.

Rates of PF

1. An employer has to make a matching contribution of 8.33 per cent to 10 per cent of wages to

employee's pension fund. Pay means salary, dearness allowance, retaining allowance, and cash value of concessions.

2. The contribution is to be diverted from the employer's share of provident fund. The central government also contributes 1.16 per cent.
3. The hospital has also to pay the contribution payable to the employee's pension fund, of the employees of the contractor.
4. If an employer defaults in payment, he has to pay a penalty as laid down.

Action to be Taken by the Employer

1. He shall ask for a declaration before employment, whether the proposed employee is a member of the PF, and if so the account number.
2. He shall prepare a contribution card in Form 3, or Form 3A, as may be appropriate. He will also prepare an employee's pension fund contribution card, for each employee.
3. He will send to the Commissioner, a consolidated return as may be specified, within 3 months of the commencement of the scheme, indicating employees who are entitled to be included in the scheme. If no employee is entitled to the scheme, he has to send a nil report.
4. He has to send to the Commissioner, by 15th of each month, returns pertaining to the previous month, showing employees qualifying to become members of the scheme, together with their declarations, and those leaving service. Nil reports are required.

5. He has to furnish to the Commissioner particulars of all branches, departments, owners, occupiers, directors, partners, managers or any person who has control of the hospital. He also shall intimate any changes, within 15 days of such change.
6. He shall deduct the employee's contribution from the wages, before paying the employee.
7. He shall pay the contributions due, within 15 days of the close of the month, to the fund.
8. He will forward to the Commissioner, within 25 days of the close of the month, a monthly consolidated statement, indicating recoveries made and contributions given. Nil returns are required.
9. The deductions and contributions in respect of each employee shall be entered in the contribution card each month. The contribution cards shall be kept in safe custody. It can be inspected by the concerned employee.
10. The employer has to maintain an inspection card, for inspection by the Commissioner or by his staff.
11. Any employee can avail of withdrawals or advances, for construction of his house, sickness, marriage of self or dependants, and higher education of his children.

Contract Labor Act

Act is applicable to hospitals in which 20 or more persons are employed on contract. This act lays down that every hospital, in which contract labor is employed, should obtain registration. If it has contractors who employ persons exceeding 20, each of such contractors must obtain registration. If the hospital terminates the contract of the contractor, the hospital is not required to absorb the employees of the contractor rendered surplus.

However, whenever the contract of the contractor is dispensed with, the employees of the contractor always claim that it is their right to get absorbed into the hospital establishment. It is therefore prudent that this is kept in mind while drawing out the contract.

Trade Union Act

The purpose of the act is to provide protection for union activities. It grants immunity against criminal prosecution for activities furthering trade union activities, or civil suits for inducing workers to break contracts. It provides that seven persons can join together and form a union, and get it registered. It must be understood that the fact that a union has been registered, does not automatically mean that the union is recognized.

Workmen's Compensation Act

The general principle is that a workman who gets injured during his work must be compensated. This is independent of the fact that no wrong doing is attributable to the employer. If such wrong doing is involved, it will come under 'tort'.

Liability of Employer for Compensation

If personal injury is caused to a workman, by accident, arising out of, and in the course of his employment, his employer to pay compensation. But the employer is not liable to pay compensation:

- ☆ In respect of injury which does not result in total or partial disablement of more than 3 days.

- In respect of injury not resulting in death or permanent disablement, directly attributable:
  1. The workman at that time, being under the influence of alcohol or drugs
  2. Willful disobedience to an order or standing instructions
  3. Willful removal of any safety guard.
- If a workman contracts a disease classified as an occupational disease, such disease will be deemed to be an accident, within the meaning of this act.

Amount of Compensation

The two relevant ingredients in this are the monthly wages of the workman and the "relevant" factor. Wages include any privilege or benefit which can be estimated in terms of money, but does not include traveling allowance or concessions, or amount paid toward provident fund. In the event of the pay of a workman, exceeding Rs 2500 per month, then it will be deemed to be Rs 2500 per month, for the purpose of this act. The relevant factor is calculated by a reference to the future earning capacity of the workman, which has been lost due to death or disablement. While the injury or degree of disablement is testified by the medical authorities, the actual quantum of compensation is decided by the boards, constituted for this purpose. As a guideline, the compensation payable is given below:

Where Death Results

Minimum is Rs 50000. The amount is equal to 50 per cent of the monthly wages, multiplied by the relevant factor, or Rs 50000 whichever is more.

Where Permanent Total Disability Results

An amount equal to 60 per cent of the monthly wages multiplied by the relevant factor or Rs 60000 whichever is more.

Where Permanent Partial Disablement Occurs

A percentage of compensation, which would have been payable, if the injury was total.

When Temporary Disablement Occurs

25 per cent of the monthly wages.

The amount of compensation is awarded by the boards set up under the act.

Festival and National Holidays Act

Under this act, each hospital has to give 15 days of holiday to its employees, in a calendar year. Four of these, namely Independence day, Republic day, Workers day (1st of May), and Gandhi Jayanti (2nd October) are national holidays, and so are compulsory. The dates of the other 9 holidays, are to be finalized in consultation with the employees. The list of holidays, are required to be finalized by November for the next calendar year, and has to be sent to the labor officer for approval. And after approval, it has to be displayed on the notice board.

In this chapter, we have dealt with the laws pertaining to organizations in general, and so applicable to hospitals. The income tax act is also applicable, but not dealt with, as its terms are already well known. The laws which are particularly and exclusively applicable to hospitals, are dealt with in the next chapter.

Chapter 22
Laws Applicable to Hospitals–II

In the previous chapter we dealt with laws applicable to organizations and so applicable to hospitals also. In this chapter, we are dealing with laws applicable specifically to hospitals. They are:

- ☆ Hospital Act.
- ☆ Nursing Homes Act.
- ☆ Consumer Protection Act.
- ☆ Indian Medical Council Act.
- ☆ Indian Nursing Council Act.
- ☆ The Pharmacy Act.

- ☆ Medical Termination of Pregnancy Act.
- ☆ Transplantation of Human Organs Act.
- ☆ Birth and Death Registration Act.

Hospital Acts

As health is a state subject, a number of laws have been passed by the states regarding registration of hospitals. Basically all hospitals have to be registered with the local bodies (Panchayats, Municipalities, and Corporations). All hospitals in the voluntary sector, or non-governmental organizations in the field of health care, have to be registered, under the Societies Registration Act.

Nursing Homes Act

There are a large number of state laws regulating Nursing Homes. The object of these laws is, to provide for registration of Nursing Homes, to enable inspection of nursing homes, and to provide provisions regarding registration and inspection. Usually, the rules framed under these acts provide for application for registration, fees chargeable, and forms of registration certificate.

It is a sad commentary, that in India, the orders issued in this regard are seldom fully complied with. The monitoring of nursing homes remains to be lax.

Consumer Protection Act

Earlier this act was considered not applicable to the medical profession, and disputes regarding medical negligence, was filed under IPC or the Law of Torts. But a ruling in 1992, by the National Consumer Disputes Redressal Commission, has included medical services under the act. Under this act the following definitions have been given:

Consumer

The patient is a consumer, if he pays for the services, or is liable for payment. So government hospitals are outside the purview of this act.

Deficiency

It is any fault, imperfection, shortcoming or inadequacy in the quality, nature and manner of providing medical care.

Service

Includes medical service of any kind, but excludes free service. It also excludes personal service. Though it was argued that a doctor's service is of a personal nature, it was ruled that his service cannot be termed as personal service, as there is no element of master-servant relationship in it.

Time Limitations

Complaints must be filed within three years of the complaint having risen. At the district forum, the case has to be heard within three months of being filed.

Levels

The national commission hears complaints of compensation above 10 lakh rupees. The state commission, deals with claims above 5 lakh rupees, and the district commission deals with claims up to 5 lakh rupees. The redressal forums have judicial powers of a civil court, and so can summon witnesses, and demand production of documents.

The key grievance of the medical fraternity is that there is no provision to have medical expert on the forums. A provision is under consideration, to provide an independent expert in the commission.

Indian Medical Council Act

The act provides for establishment of a Medical Council of India (MCI), and for a register to register doctors of modern medicine. The act lays down the code of conduct for medical practitioners, and regulates medical education. State medical councils established under the act, have the same function as the central medical council, except that recognition of teaching hospitals, which is centrally governed by the MCI. The act was first promulgated in 1956, and has been amended in 1964 and 1993. It gives the MCI the sole authority to grant recognition to medical colleges, to increase or reduce the course capacity of these medical colleges, and to sanction post graduate courses.

Indian Medical Register

The Council shall cause to be maintained in the prescribed manner, a register of medical practitioners to be known as the Indian Medical Register, which shall contain the names of all persons, who are for the time being enrolled on any State Medical Register, and who possess any of the recognized medical qualifications.

It shall be the duty of the Registrar of the Council, to keep the Indian Medical Register in accordance with the provisions of this Act, and of any orders made by the Council, from time to time, to revise the register and publish it in the Gazette of India and in such other manner as may be prescribed.

Registration in the Indian Medical Register

The Registrar of the Council, may, on receipt of the report of registration of a person in a State Medical Register or on application made in the prescribed manner by any such person, enter his name in the Indian Medical Register, provided that the Registrar is satisfied, that the person concerned possesses a recognized medical qualification.

Removal from the Register

If the name of any person enrolled on a State Medical Register, is removed there from in pursuance of any power conferred by or under any law relating to medical practitioners for the time being in force in any State, the Council shall direct the removal of the name of such person, from the Indian Medical Register.

Where the name of any person has been removed from a State Medical Register on the ground of professional misconduct, or any other ground, he may appeal in the prescribed manner.

Offences and Professional Misconduct of Doctors

For certain offences, a doctor can be temporarily struck off from the medical register. Some of them are enumerated below:

- Adultery, or improper conduct, with a patient, or a member of his family.
- Issuing, false medical certificates.
- Conviction by a Court of Law, for offences involving moral factors.
- Selling Schedule poisons.
- Performing, illegal abortions, or surgeries.

- Advertising the services of an institution, run by a physician.
- Using unusually large sign boards, or fixing sign boards at places other than that of his residence or practice.
- Disclosing secrets, of a patient.
- Performing, operations without consent.
- Using agents or incentives to procure business.
- Claiming qualifications or medical degrees, he does not possess.

Indian Nursing Council Act

This act lays down the educational standards and requirements for the registration of nurses. It extends to the whole of India, except the State of Jammu and Kashmir.

Indian Nurses Register

The Council shall cause to be maintained, in the prescribed manner, a Register of Nurses, Midwives, Auxiliary Nurse Midwives and Health Visitors to be known as the Indian Nurses Register, which shall contain the names of all persons who are for the time being, enrolled on any State register. It shall be the duty of the Secretary of the Council, to keep the Indian Nurses Register, in accordance with the provisions of this Act, and from time to time, to revise the register and publish it in the Gazette of India, and in such other manner as may be prescribed.

Recognized Qualifications

Certificates (including senior and junior certificates), Diplomas or Degrees in Nursing, issued by any of the recognized authorities, The recognized qualifications are listed centrally. In case of a foreign qualification, cases are dealt with on a case to case basis.

The Pharmacy Act

This Act, is to regulate the functioning of pharmacies, and drug stores, and deals with the professional pharmacists. A hospital has to acquire a drug license, if it sells drugs across the counter. The dispensing of drugs can only be done, by a registered pharmacist. The act provides for setting up of a Pharmacy Council, with a registrar who will act as the secretary of the council. It shall be the duty of the Registrar of the Central Council to keep the Central Register in accordance with the orders made by the Central Council, and from time to time to revise the Central Register, and publish it in the Gazette of India.

Registration in the Central Register

The Registrar of the Central Council shall, on receipt of the report of registration of a person in the State Register, enter his name in the Central Register.

Medical Termination of Pregnancy Act

The Act provides for the termination of certain pregnancies by registered medical practitioners, and for matters connected therewith or incidental thereto.

Maintenance of Admission Register

1. Every approved hospital or owner of the approved place shall maintain a register in form III for recording there in the details of the admissions of women for the termination of their pregnancies, and keep such register for a period of five years, from the end of the calendar year it relates to.

2. The entries in the Admission Register shall be made serially and a fresh serial shall be started at the commencement of each calendar year, and the serial number of the particular year shall be distinguished from the serial number of other years, by mentioning the year against the serial number, for example, serial number 5 of 1972 and serial number 5 of 1973, shall be mentioned as 5/1972 and 5/1973.
3. Admission Register shall be a secret document and the information contained therein as to the name and other particulars of the pregnant woman, shall not be disclosed to any person.

Approval of a Place

No place shall be approved, unless the Government is satisfied that termination of pregnancies, may be done therein under safe and hygienic conditions; and has the following facilities:

A gynecology examination/labor table, resuscitation and sterilization equipment, drugs and parental fluid, back up facilities for treatment of shock, and facilities for transportation; And in the case of second trimester pregnancy up to 20 weeks of pregnancy, an operation table, and instruments for performing abdominal or gynecological surgery.

Experience and Training for Doctors

For doing medical termination of pregnancy, a registered medical practitioner shall have one or more of the following experience or training in Gynecology and Obstetrics, namely;

- ☆ In the case of a medical practitioner, who is registered in a State Medical Register: if he has completed six months of house surgency in gynecology and obstetrics; or if he had experience at any hospital for a period of not less than one year, in the practice of obstetrics and gynecology; or he has assisted a registered medical practitioner in the performance of twenty-five cases of medical termination of pregnancy, of which at least five have been performed independently, in a hospital established or maintained, or a training institute approved for this purpose by the government.
- ☆ A medical practitioner, who has been registered in a State Medical Register, and who holds a post-graduate degree or diploma in Gynecology and Obstetrics. The experience or training gained during the course of such degree or diploma would be adequate.

Human Organ Transplantation Act

The transplantation of an organ from one body to another is known as the organ transplant. The person, who gives the organ, is called the Donor, while the one who receives it is called the Recipient. Organ transplant is done, to replace the recipient's damaged organ, with the working organ of the donor, so that the recipient could function normally. The person who is donating the organ (donor), could either be a living person or a deceased person.

Organ Transplantation is a boon to medical industry, as it has helped in saving the lives of those, who would have died otherwise. There are various laws that are to be followed while conducting the organ transplant. Kidney, Eyes, Liver, Heart, Lung, Pancreas, Small bowel, and Skin etc. are some of the organs that can be donated for an organ transplant.

Due to inefficient and corrupt healthcare system, illegal trafficking of organ is really high in India. To stop illegal organ transplant, Indian Government has come up with a 1994 law that criminalizes Organ Sales. The Human Organs Transplant Act 1994, has laid down certain rules and regulations, that are to be followed while conducting organ transplant.

Organ transplant law does not allow exchange of money between the donor and the recipient. According to the Act, the unrelated donor has to file an affidavit in the court of a magistrate, stating that the organ is being donated out of affection. After which the donor has to undergo number of tests, before the actual transplant takes place. Then the case goes to Authorization or Ethics committee, who has to approve the transplantation before the operation can be performed. The operation can only be done, by doctors who are specially authorized to perform human trans plantation. The Authorization Committee set up for the purpose ensures that all the documents required under the act, have been supplied. If it is found that the money has been exchanged in the process, then both the recipient as well as the donor is considered as offenders under the law.

According to the Indian law, organ sales are banned and therefore no foreigner can usually get a local donor. Human organ transplant laws are very strict in India and the penalty incurred for organ trade, is also very high.

According to the Indian Law, close relatives of recipient like parents, children, brothers, sisters, and spouse can donate the organ without government clearance. But all other relatives, who wish to donate the organ, need to appear before the Authorization Committee for clearance, and only after its approval and clearance, can the organ be transplanted.

Birth and Death Registration Act

In case of births in a hospital, it shall be the duty of the hospital, to inform the local authority, the birth of the child in the prescribed form, within the prescribed period. The prescribed form must be handed over to the section concerned, and a receipt obtained in a register. Where the birth of any child has been registered without a name, the parent or guardian of such child shall within the prescribed period give information regarding the name of the child to the registrar either orally or in writing and thereupon the Registrar shall enter such a name in the register and initial and date the entry. If the hospital has not informed the local body during the prescribed period, then depending upon the period of delay, the hospital has to take action, as prescribed by the local body.

In case of deaths the hospital has to inform the local body nearest to the hospital, the death, in the prescribed form, giving a copy to the nearest relative of the deceased. This form must contain the cause of death, by the doctor certifying death, giving his name, address, qualifications and medical registration number. But in cases of brought in dead, where the patient had died before the arrival of the patient to the hospital, then the hospital has to inform the local body to which the patient belongs. Hence, before handing over the body, the particulars of the local body to which the deceased belonged, must be obtained and kept on record.

Holding Stock of Narcotic Drugs

Drugs like morphia and pethidine, though habit forming, and other similar habit forming drugs have clinical value, and cannot be replaced by other drugs. But, because of the possibility of its misuse, special rules have been made for stocking it.

1. It has to be applied for by a registered medical practitioner, separately, justifying the need to hold stocks, and its monthly requirement.
2. This is verified by a representative of the Drug Controller, who issues a license for this, giving the monthly amount which can be purchased, at any one time, and the maximum stock which can be held.
3. This license is issued to a doctor only, in his name.
4. The doctor who holds the license is bound to keep the drugs under his personal custody.
5. The drug can only be issued to the patient, by the doctor who is holding the license. The quantity, issued must be supported by an entry in the case sheet of the patient concerned.

Miscellaneous

Under this section, certain legal matters a hospital administrator has to deal with, in his daily functioning, are briefly summarized.

Leave

Leave with wages are different from holidays. Holidays are off-days granted by the employer, and on these days the entire hospital is closed, except for emergency services and inpatient services, while on leave, except for the person on leave, the entire hospital is functioning.

Annual Leave

The leave entitlement in a hospital is laid down in the terms and conditions of employment, or according to the conditions of contract. As per the Industrial Act, any employee who has worked in a hospital for 240 days, or more in the calendar year, is entitled to annual leave with wages, But the entitled leave is to be availed of, in the subsequent year. Holidays can be prefixed or suffixed to the leave. An employee who is dismissed or discharged, or superannuates or dies, he or his nominee, is entitled to wages in lieu of the entitled leave. Unless so specified or contracted, an employee is entitled to one day leave for every twenty days he has worked in the previous calendar year, subject to the provision of 240 days work in the calendar year.

To avail of annual leave, an employee has to apply in writing 15 days before the day he wants to avail of his leave, giving reasons why he wants to avail of leave. The dictionary meaning of leave is "permission". Employee can only avail of leave, *after obtaining leave and being granted leave*. The mere fact that an employee is entitled to leave, does not give him the right to avail of leave, *without being granted leave*. However it is incumbent on the employer to grant leave if entitled, as far as possible, and denial of leave must be on bona-fide grounds. Surrendering of leave for cash payment is governed under the conditions of service or contract. However if entitled leave was not granted during the calendar year, even though requested for, such leave can be availed of in the next calendar year. When accumulation of leave is permitted, the maximum leave which can be accumulated is laid down, in the conditions of service.

Casual Leave

In order to cater for emergencies, an employee is permitted casual leave. The quantum of casual leave is calculated at the rate of one day casual leave for each completed month of service, and cannot be carried over beyond 31st of December. As this leave is meant for emergencies, there is no compulsion that such leave must be granted, because of its entitlement.

Sick Leave

In case of sickness, it is not possible to insist on 15 days notice. But applications for such leave, has to be accompanied by a valid medical certificate. The quantum of leave, and how much on full pay or on half pay, is as per the conditions of service. If the sickness period is over and above the sick leave entitlement, the break in service can be regularized, by adjustment against entitlement of annual leave or leave without pay. On return from sick leave, an employee is required to bring a fitness certificate.

Obligation of Employee

If absence is not covered by grant of leave, this constitutes a break in service. It is the duty of the employee, to get this break in service regularized.

Procedure for Disciplinary Action

Though the Industrial Dispute Act does not lay down any definite procedure for awarding punishment, such a procedure has evolved from the judgment of Courts of Law. Broadly speaking the following steps are to be followed in such cases:

- ☆ Charge sheet
- ☆ Holding of a Domestic Enquiry
- ☆ Report of the enquiry officer
- ☆ Show cause notice
- ☆ Examination of record of service
- ☆ Order of punishment.

The first obligation of the employee is, to obey the lawful orders of the employer. Misconduct makes an employee liable to disciplinary action. Misconduct means bad behavior. It implies wrongful intention, and not a mere error of judgment. It does not necessarily involve corruption or criminal intent. An omission to do what is expected of an employee is misconduct, but if the omission is directed intentionally to cause mischief or loss, it is willful misconduct. The term "misconduct" usually implies an act done willfully, with wrong intention, as applied to professional matters. Some of the following acts are considered as misconduct:

1. Any act or conduct which is prejudicial to the interest or reputation of the employer.
2. Any act or conduct incompatible with the peaceful discharge of duty.
3. Any act or conduct of a worker, which makes it unsafe for the employer to retain him.

4. An act or conduct which is grossly immoral.
5. An act or conduct that makes it impossible for the employer, to trust him.
6. Use of filthy language.
7. Insulting behavior or insubordination
8. Habitual neglect of duties, or habitual coming late to work.
9. Theft, fraud or dishonest.
10. Illegal strike
11. Absence with out leave, disobedience to orders
12. Disrespect or assaulting superiors.
13. Damage to property or disreputable outside conduct.
14. Delinquencies like telling lies, disloyalty, or corruption.

Charge Sheet

It is a memorandum of acts of omission or commission, which is punishable, alleged o have been committed by the worker. The charge sheet must give the employee a clear idea of the accusation against him. If the charge is late attendance then the word "habitual" must be included. Similarly in neglect, the words "gross", may be essential, the charge sheet should also mention the particulars of time, place, and manner of the incident to make the charge specific. In a charge sheet, any document or record which is relied upon must be disclosed. Normally, the charge sheet, must be in simple clear language, which an employee can understand. It must satisfy the following conditions:

- The charge sheet must specify the charges, in clear language, with full particulars.
- It must disclose the offence or misconduct with which an employee is charged.
- The language used must be precise and not vague.
- It will not be enough to state that an employee is willfully slowing down his performance, but it must have particulars how the slowing down was done.
- It should not contain unnecessary matters.
- The use of abbreviations like "etc" or "any other documents" must be avoided.
- Whenever it is necessary to give the time of the event, the word "about" must be added.
- In case of disobedience, the order disobeyed must be mentioned. Saying "I will not do it", is not disobedience, and the order must be disobeyed within a reasonable period.
- In case of theft, the particulars of the goods stolen must be given.
- In case of misappropriation, all particulars regarding the amount misappropriated must be given.
- When the charge is falsification of accounts, the details of the particulars where falsification was done must be given.
- The charge sheet must contain all essential particulars.

Service of Charge Sheet

Serving of a charge sheet is an essential ingredient of further proceedings of the domestic enquiry. The commonest form of serving a charge sheet is by personal service. The charge sheet must be handed over to the employee and his signature obtained in token of having received it. In case he refuses to receive it, or refuses to sign in token of having received it, an endorsement must be made to that effect in presence of two witnesses. However, if an employee wants the charge sheet made out in a local language or Hindi, it must be done.

Powers to Suspend, Pending an Enquiry

The point to remember is that suspension cannot be given as a form of punishment. Ordinarily it is better to avoid it. If suspended, the employee has to be paid 50 per cent of his wages for the first 90 days, and 75 per cent of his pay, thereafter.

Domestic Enquiry

The procedure to be followed in a domestic enquiry is to inform the employee the time and place of the enquiry. A domestic enquiry officer must be appointed, and during enquiry, the employer or his representative, must lead the evidence against the employee, giving him, opportunity to cross examine, and at the end the employee must be asked if he wants to give any explanation in his defense. After giving the accused a fair chance to be heard, the enquiry officer must record his findings, based on the evidence presented.

Report of the Enquiry Officer

When the domestic enquiry is over the report is to be

submitted. Such reports come for consideration by tribunals and courts of law, and so should be carefully written. It is always prudent that reasons be given for the findings, and the findings are based on the particulars in the charge sheet, and the evidence presented. No extraneous matters must come into play. It is mandatory that a copy of the domestic enquiry should be provided to the accused.

Punishment

For any proven misconduct, a punishment is mandatory. It is imperative that strict discipline be maintained in hospitals, as they deal with life and death. The power of punishment is that of the management. Labor courts have no power to interfere with management's orders, when the misconduct has been proved. The exception is that the punishment is so misappropriate, that a perversity can be inferred, or it is to victimize. The adjudicating authority has been given powers under the Industrial Dispute Act, to interfere with the quantum of punishment. However before awarding punishment, the employee's record service must be examined.

Resignation

Resignation is a mode of putting an end to the service contract by the employee. A notice of resignation has to be given by the employee, usually one months notice. However the employee can withdraw his resignation within the notice period. If the employee has given notice or surrendered his pay in lieu of, normally the resignation has to be accepted.

Chapter 23
Quality Assurance

The whole purpose of the book is to highlight the role of supporting services, in maintaining quality in hospital care. So to conclude, a look at the ways available to assess quality in the care provided in hospitals becomes imperative. The theory and practice of health care are often not the same. In theory it must be possible to provide the best possible treatment and care for the patients, in a well managed hospital. In practice, we cannot do so, however well managed the hospital is. So with the best of intentions, really good hospitals can fall below the standards, for a variety of reasons. Hence the necessity for quality assurance procedures, to ensure that hospitals have a system for regular checking, to determine if the hospital is adhering to the standards.

The term quality assurance is of recent origin, and has replaced "medical audit", which is basically a study of medical records in retrospect. In this context quality is defined as adherence to standards and criteria based on current knowledge, and experience. Quality assurance is a planned program, which objectively monitors and evaluates the performance of medical practitioners, to identify opportunities for improvement, and to correct inadequacies. Quality control cannot be a one time retrospective medical audit, nor can it be a periodical enquiry system into incidents of negligence.

There are a number of methods and techniques to measure quality of medical care. In essence it must have the following ingredients:

- ☆ It should be a systemic ongoing activity.
- ☆ Emphasis should be on monitoring for improvement, rather than fault finding.
- ☆ It must be system orientated, rather than picking out individual inefficiencies.
- ☆ It must not be "best care at any cost", but "reasonable standard of care at reasonable cost".
- ☆ All the variables of the system namely input, process and output must be appraised. Medical professionals must agree on optimum input, including structural infrastructure.
- ☆ It must look at all aspects of care, quality of technical care, quality of the art of care, and the quality of amenities of care. Technical care involves correctness of diagnosis, appropriate therapeutic regimen, which assures a defined clinical outcome. The art of care relates to the interaction with the patient/relatives, and includes attitude, courtesy,

communication and professional conduct. Amenity of care is assurance of a good hospital environment, such as cleanliness, hospital linen, privacy, lack of noise, and appetizing food.

Purpose of Quality Assurance

It is three fold:

1. Help patients, including potential patients, by improving quality.
2. Assess competence of the medical team, and act as an incentive to update knowledge and skills, as well as prevent future mistakes.
3. Bring to light the deficiencies and help in taking corrective action.

Types of Quality Assurance

It can be broadly divided into external and internal quality assurance. External quality assurance is setting up of standards by an independent outside authority, covering wide areas of health care, and then getting it assessed by independent assessors. Internal quality assurance is essentially a local exercise, where the work of physicians is subject to a confidential review by their peers, designed to improve patient care and self evaluation.

Method

Quality assurance program can be either concurrent or retrospective

Concurrent Review

It is used routinely in the form of daily administrative rounds. It also can be made as a part of the daily clinical rounds. It is done while the patient is in the ward, and so, it oversees things as it happen day-to-day. The patient's medical records are perused, the patients clinical progress is determined, enquiries are made from the patient about his treatment and diet, the nurses record is looked into, and the housekeeping activities, including sanitation is assessed. Any deficiencies are corrected on the spot, and orders issued for remedial action. The discharge analyses action, often carried out in the medical record department can be shifted to the wards, monitored by a senior nurse, usual problems being, verbal orders given by the doctor not endorsed on the case sheet, medication errors, and duplication of lab tests. Analysis of medical records, immediately on discharge, will enable the final diagnosis being recorded, before the record is sent to MRD, for filing. This assures accuracy of information in the medical records.

Retrospective Review

Quality assurance programs require a step by step approach. There are three fundamental requisites for a retrospective audit, namely a good medical record; established criteria for diagnosis, investigation and treatment, as well as involvement of the medical staff.

1. Good medical record consists of admission office records, doctor's notes, nurse's report, and notes by supportive services (lab investigation reports, radiographic reports, and special investigation reports). The medical record must be sequentially filed, and a "face sheet" affixed to each record, before it is given for evaluation. Ideally this is done by the medical record librarian, but can be taught to a nursing assistant.

2. Establishment of criteria for diagnosis, investigation, and treatment by a group of senior consultants. Variations from the criteria and standards are only acceptable, when a peer review attributes the variation, to the patient's condition.
3. Common standards. A few applicable to India are given as a guide:
   (*a*) Gross death rate: 3 to 5 per cent
   (*b*) Net death rate: Not to exceed 2.5 per cent
   (*c*) Anesthesia death rate: Not to exceed 1 per 5000 anesthesia given.
   (*d*) Post-operative death rate: Less than 1 per cent.
   (*e*) Maternal death rate: Not to exceed 0.25 per cent
   (*f*) Neonatal death rate: Not to exceed 2 per cent
   (*g*) Hospital infection rate: Less than 4 per cent of all admitted cases.
   (*h*) Post-operative infection rate: Not to exceed 1 to 2 per cent
   (*i*) Caesarian section rate: Not to exceed 10 to 15 per cent
4. Securing involvement of Medical staff. The doctors and nurses must be prepared to subject themselves to evaluation by their peer group. They must be convinced that quality assurance program evaluation is not a fault finding exercise. It must be fully supported by the top management.

Mechanics of Quality Assurance

Records of patients are initially examined with the help of MRD staff. Records which confirm to the laid down criteria are not examined any further. Records which show a discrepancy is laid before the committee. The records can be distributed equally to each member of the committee before the committee formally meets. Each member writes down his observations regarding diagnosis, treatment, complications and outcome of treatment. These are then reviewed by the committee. After review, important discrepancies are informed to all departments, without identifying the individual physician. If a few doctors account for most of the deficiencies, the head of the departments requested to meet them and discuss the problem.

Techniques of Quality Measurement

Some of the techniques are given below:

- ☆ *Accreditation*. This is becoming the ideal technique. It is supportive assessment, not only to identify deficiencies, but also suggestions regarding improvement.
- ☆ *Credentialing*. A doctors credentials (qualification, registration, specific training, experience and current competency), is verified before he is allowed to function independently.
- ☆ Enquiry into complaints by patients.

Committees

Quality assurance activities are best undertaken by standing committees.

- ☆ *Medical audit*: Each department must carry out its own medical audit, and the minutes should be available to the quality assurance committee.

- *Nursing audit*: Nursing Superintend must carry out monthly nursing audit.
- *Patient Satisfaction Surveys.*
- *Statistics*: The QA department must compile statistics for the following with the help of MRD:
  - (*a*) No of admissions, bed occupancy, surgical procedures, length of stay, in-patient turnover, out-patient visits, mortality rates.
  - (*b*) *Practitioner profile*: Outpatient load, admissions, surgeries, complications, deaths, patient satisfaction.
  - (*c*) *Activity audit*: Use of surgical time, delayed or cancelled surgeries, incidents of delay in getting investigation report, equipment out of order, non-availability of blood/drugs.

Index

Hospital Supporting Services & Systems